Forty-Five Meditations on
Loneliness
and Revelation
A Study of the Sacred

Forty-Five Meditations on
Loneliness
and Revelation
A Study of the Sacred

Brendan Myers

BOOKS

Winchester, UK
Washington, USA

First published by O-Books, 2010
O Books is an imprint of John Hunt Publishing Ltd., The Bothy, Deershot Lodge, Park Lane, Ropley,
Hants, SO24 0BE, UK
office1@o-books.net
www.o-books.com

Distribution in:	South Africa
	Stephan Phillips (pty) Ltd
UK and Europe	Email: orders@stephanphillips.com
Orca Book Services Ltd	Tel: 27 21 4489839 Telefax: 27 21 4479879
Home trade orders	Text copyright: Brendan Myers 2009
tradeorders@orcabookservices.co.uk	
Tel: 01235 465521 Fax: 01235 465555	ISBN: 978 1 84694 355 3
Export orders	Design: Stuart Davies
exportorders@orcabookservices.co.uk	
Tel: 01235 465516 or 01235 465517	All rights reserved. Except for brief quotations
Fax: 01235 465555	in critical articles or reviews, no part of this
	book may be reproduced in any manner
USA and Canada	without prior written permission from the
NBN	publishers.
custserv@nbnbooks.com	
Tel: 1 800 462 6420 Fax: 1 800 338 4550	The rights of Brendan Myers as author have
	been asserted in accordance with the
Australia and New Zealand	Copyright, Designs and Patents Act 1988.
Brumby Books	
sales@brumbybooks.com.au	A CIP catalogue record for this book is
Tel: 61 3 9761 5535 Fax: 61 3 9761 7095	available from the British Library.
Far East (offices in Singapore, Thailand,	
Hong Kong, Taiwan)	
Pansing Distribution Pte Ltd	Printed in the UK by CPI Antony Rowe
kemal@pansing.com	Printed in the USA by Offset Paperback Mfrs,
Tel: 65 6319 9939 Fax: 65 6462 5761	Inc

We operate a distinctive and ethical publishing philosophy in all
areas of its business, from its global network of authors to
production and worldwide distribution.

CONTENTS

Preface, Acknowledgement, and Dedication   1

The Cairn   5
The Problem   8
The Night Watch   13
The City   16
The Individual   19
The Man on the Bus   23
A Clarification   25
The Waterfront   28
The Distant Shore   31
The Lover's Dilemma   33
The Solitude of God   37
The Wisdom of Lucretius   41
The Great Silence   43
The Towers   49
The Concert   52
The Ripples on the Water   54
"I am Here!"   57
A Digression   65
"This is Who I Am!"   70
The Invocation   72
The Way That Can Be Spoken   76
"And What I Am Is Beautiful!"   79
Another Digression   83
The Will   86
The First of All Moral Judgments   89
The Examined Life   93
The Terrorist   95
The Personal Task   99
The Social Task   101
The Green Man   103

The Parasite   108

The Razor's Edge   110

The Mist   112

The Vision   113

The Message   118

"Is Anyone Else Out There?"   120

The Musician   123

The Camp Fire   127

The Harbour   130

The Lovers' Gaze   135

The Festival   143

The Artist   149

The Beautiful and the Good   153

The Ocean   159

The Turning of the Wheel   161

Bibliography   164

Part One of a Series

Preface, Acknowledgement, and Dedication

I've lived entirely alone for most of my adult life so far, and most of the time I have preferred it that way. But around ten years ago, an event in my life which I'll not describe here made me speculate that loneliness might be more than a social situation: it might be an existential condition of human life. To understand loneliness properly, and to understand relationships properly, I realised I could not turn to others: I had to go deep within my own mind. I examined the times in which I greatly desired companionship, and examined the many foolish things I did to gain and to keep that companionship. Four elementary propositions emerged from all that introspection. And a simple ten-page explanation of those propositions, originally intended as a small part of a different project, quickly blossomed into the book you now hold in your hands.

In various places in this text, I use quotations and stories from people I know, rather than from published philosophical texts, even when excellent texts are available. I do this in order to drive home the point that everyone is capable of philosophical reflection. Philosophy happens not only in university classrooms: it happens everywhere. After all, Socrates did philosophy in marketplaces, public streets, and at dinner parties with his friends! And I've never met someone who couldn't formulate and logically examine a serious philosophical question, and a serious answer to that question. I also believe that our most important philosophical and spiritual ideas emerge from conversations, dialogues, and relationships. This book, therefore, is partially the product of a hundred conversations I had with a great many thoughtful and good-hearted people from around the world, over many years.

At the time of writing, our world has fallen deep into the worst economic depression in almost a hundred years. Despite huge government "bailout" payments, and the confident pronouncements of politicians, real signs of recovery are not yet apparent. A severe (and under-reported) planet-wide food shortage is in progress. The extreme storms of global warming and climate change are displacing or killing millions of people around the world. The price of the most important energy resource, petroleum, continues to inflate rapidly, contributing to world poverty. Fundamentalist forms of religion are veritably feeding the flames of fear, xenophobia, racism, sexism, warfare, and international terrorism. And deadly pandemic diseases, such as AIDS, continue to ruin whole societies, especially in the world's most populous and poorest countries. A kind of hopelessness and despair is settling on many people, even in prosperous countries. More people in Canada, the USA, and Europe die from suicide now than from traffic accidents. One of the philosophical results of this situation is that social and political principles which were once treated as iron-clad laws of nature are increasingly coming under scrutiny and doubt. Some have been plainly refuted by the facts. Yet it is precisely in such times of crisis that people examine and re-think their first-order beliefs. As the philosopher Hegel wrote: "Minerva's Owl spreads her wings by the fall of night." My duty, as a philosopher and as a thinking human being, is to contribute to this re-thinking process in a useful and enlightening way. I hope to help people think and speak peacefully, rationally, and productively with each other about what human life's true priorities should be. My hope is that if we can do this, then we will prevent crises like these, or respond to them better, and create more socially just societies, and live more fulfilling lives. I therefore thank you, dear reader, for sparing some of your hard earned money to buy this little book. I hope it contributes positively to your own thinking on the things that matter most to you, and to those who are close to you.

For a work that features loneliness as such a prominent theme, it's difficult for me to decide who deserves to be thanked in print. Anyone I name here might think I was saying they are among the most miserable sad-sacks I know. But I feel that I owe thanks to a number of people who have benefited me during the time this book was written. First, I thank the many people who organized and attended four public talks where I presented some of the ideas laid out here before you. These talks, in Salisbury England, Milan Italy, Pigeon Lake Alberta, and Ottawa Ontario, gave me many excellent criticisms and suggestions which refined and improved the argument. Of individuals, I owe my first thanks to Sian Reid, for the generous gift of a place to live for the year during which much of this book was written. I'm grateful to her and to others for many good conversations which often helped me clarify my thoughts: my siblings Bridgit and Ciaran, and my friends Philip Carr-Gomm, Emily Rose Michaud, Victoria Maier, Amanda Hyde, Helmut Foster, Kelly Lynn, NaTasha Bertrand, Juniper Cox, Austin Lawrence and Maryanne Pearce. The latter two friends deserve special thanks for giving me the idea of producing this work as a series of short books, instead of as one impossibly large single volume. Once again, a book of mine is being written (in part) on their dining room table.

But I feel I must give special gratitude to my good and beautiful friend Jane Estelle Trombley. Thinking and writing philosophically about loneliness for an entire year cannot help but have an effect on one's emotional life. Jane's comments helped turn frustrated thinking into productive thinking, and her good humour and her love kept me from falling into the very loneliness that I was writing of. I therefore dedicate this humble work to her.

Brendan Myers
Ottawa, Ontario, Canada
August 2009.

3

§ 1. The Cairn

If you have never been to the high arctic of northern Canada, you might imagine it as a cold and empty landscape of ice and wind and snow. Short and stubby plants like mosses and lichens are the only growing things here. Beneath your feet you find tundra, or bare rock, instead of soil. Small crawling insects cling to the darker surfaces of boulders, where just enough sunlight can be concentrated to make it warm enough. Most of the year, everything is covered in snow and ice, and appears lifeless in an absolute sense. If you are only visiting, and you don't live and work there, the landscape would surely appear very bleak, very empty, very lonely.

On a ridge just above us stands a long forgotten lonely cairn of stones. It is roughly in the shape of a human being, with two piles of stones at the base to represent legs, a bulky stone or two which bridges them representing the body, a long thin wedge-like stone above that representing outstretched arms, and a last tall stone at the top to represent the head. This kind of cairn is called an Inukshuk, and the tradition of building them belongs to the Inuit people of northern Canada.

Jean Briggs, an anthropologist who lived for two years with an Inuk family in Chantrey Inlet, in what is now the territory of Nunavut, described what these cairns mean to the people who build them.

I was awed by the granite silence of the shores between which we paddled. The dip of the paddle, and the quiet remarks of my companions were the only sounds. The stone fingers of cairns protruding into the gray sky to me accentuated the emptiness, the loneliness of the scene. But the Utku build cairns to *lessen* the loneliness, to create company for themselves. My companions knew the builders of many of the cairns; some had been built by people already familiar to me as well. (Briggs, *Never in Anger*, pg. 35, emphasis hers.)

According to this first-hand account, the Inuit people build cairns and Inukshuks and other small monuments in order to make the landscape less lonely. The Inuit hunter or trader does not see himself traveling in an abandoned, desolate wasteland, as long as he occasionally passes an Inukshuk on his way.

When I first read Briggs' description of the Inukshuk I was strongly reminded of the Neolithic monuments of the west of Ireland, where I lived and worked for several years. The Burren, in county Clare, is a great expanse of bare rock, with long straight cracks called grykes in which the barest mosses and most fragile flowers cling to life. The region of Connemara, in west county Galway, is a patchwork of wind-battered mountains and wave-battered coasts. Some fields are bare rocks with patches of rough grass like pools in the depressions. Others are fields of bog and long grass, with islands of rock that emerge from below. Yet these uninviting landscapes have their monuments: long stone walls and old stone farmhouses, some of them in ruins since the Famine. There are signs of modernity here too, such as the tall pylons that carry electric wires over the long distances. Finally, there are remnants of an ancient society. We know of its existence only from archaeological discoveries: a few settlements, a few stone tools and pottery fragments, a few earthworks and field boundaries which suggest settled farming. We don't know their language or much of their history. We don't even know the name they used for themselves. But we know that they were prolific builders. They left hundreds of cairns, portal dolmen, stone circles and standing stones, and massive artificial mounds, some of them with long interior passages and large chambers with high ceilings. The largest of the stone dolmen of the west, Poulnabrone, is an artificial mound ringed by curb stones, with several upright pillar-stones arranged in a kind of wedge shape, supporting a massive cap-stone. Furthermore, like many monuments of its kind, Poulnabrone is also a tomb. In 1985 a cracked pillar-stone was removed and replaced, and during the renovations an underground chamber was discovered, which contained the mortal remains of twenty-two people.

After four and a half years in Ireland, I returned to Canada. While I was away, the government created a new territory in the far north, and called it Nunavut. The ubiquitous Inukshuk became the new territory's official emblem. But in a short time, the whole country adopted it as a new symbol of national identity. People were building their own little Inukshuks in their front yards. The Vancouver Olympic Winter Games made it their official emblem. The Inukshuk began to remind me of the Irish stone circles and portal dolmen that I visited so often. A new set of questions began to form in my mind. Did the Neolithic farmers of ancient Ireland build their monuments for the same reason that the Inuit people build Inukshuks? Could Poulnabrone have served not only as a tomb, but also as a sign of a human presence which makes the world less lonely? And could this assertion of a human presence, against a frontier of loneliness, be the force that initiates a great task: the fashioning of a worthwhile life here on Earth?

These are the kinds of questions we will explore in the meditations to follow. But as I hope we will find, they are but local examples of much more universal questions which affect everyone, even if only once in a while.

§ 2. The Problem

Human life is often profoundly lonely. A recent American study found that one quarter of all Americans have no close friends at all. This figure is more than double that which was found twenty years previously. Despite internet-based social networks that enable people to be in touch with hundreds of others, only half of the people interviewed for the study said they had someone to confide in about serious personal matters. (Shankar Vedantam, "Social Isolation Growing in U.S., Study Says" *The Washington Post*, 23 June 2006, page A03; Janet Kornblum, "Study: 25% of Americans have no one to confide in" *USA Today*, 22 June 2006.) The last United States census found that 27.2 million households, one-fourth of the total, consisted in just one person. Half a century ago, that was the case for only one-tenth of all house-holds. ("Lonely Nation", *The Associated Press*, 6 August 2006.) In Canada and other western countries, the situation appears only slightly less bad.

Although perhaps not everyone would describe himself as lonely, everyone knows what the experience of loneliness feels like. You first encountered it as an infant. Your parents put you down into your crib to sleep, or gave you to the care of others, even if only for a few hours, while they ran errands or got some sleep of their own. You felt it as a child when a parent, a sibling, a respected teacher, or a close friend wanted to spend time with someone else instead of with you. You felt it when you left your parental nest for the first time, to live on your own. You felt it when you had an argument with a loved one, and made that person angry at you for a little while. You felt it when you parted ways with a girlfriend or boyfriend, a husband or wife, even if you were the one who initiated the parting, and even if the relationship was unhealthy and *had* to end.

Most people will do nearly anything to avoid feeling lonely. If you are at home alone, you might turn on your television or the radio, even if you have no desire to watch it. The "white noise" in the background creates the illusion that there are other people nearby. It also keeps your mind busy, so that you won't have to think about anything. You might spend most of your spare hours on the internet, using the matrix of social networking sites or online role-play games to distract yourself from your solitude. You might even call a late-night phone sex line. The interaction with other users gives these services the impression of human reality. Similarly you might post a video of yourself to the internet, or start up a regular 'blog'. If you do something particularly entertaining, controversial, or embarrassing for all to see, then you might gain a large audience in a short amount of time. You might become so immersed in the online world that it becomes more real to you than the rest of your life. Your sense of self worth might become attached to the way online strangers respond to the things you say and do. I know people who check their email every three minutes, using their mobile phones, just in case someone wrote to them. But virtual reality, however convincing and impressive, is not reality. An online chat room is simply no substitute for a face-to-face conversation.

In search of real conversation, you might go to parties, bars, night clubs, concerts, house parties or other places where people gather. But in crowds you get to see all the relationships other people have with each other which you are not a part of, and are not invited to join. You might talk to everyone and anyone, about everything and nothing, and dominate the conversation to remain the centre of attention at all times. You might gossip about people, and gather attention to yourself by acting as a provider of social information. But if you socially manipulate and control your friends in order to keep them close, you will eventually gain their resentment, and lose them anyway. Alternatively, you might try to escape from loneliness with alcohol, or by gorging yourself with food. But once the giddiness wears off and the hangover sets in, and once the food is gone and the hunger returns, loneliness also returns. In the process you might gain various health problems like obesity or addiction, which in turn give you still more reason to feel isolated from others.

You might turn to the glamour of movies and television, and immerse yourself in the lives of the people portrayed there. But mass media entertainment can only offer a fantasy world. No matter how intimately you may feel you know the characters, they are not real people, and they are not engaged in any substantial interaction with you. Even the news in the mass media is partially 'unreal', because of the way it selects, ignores, exaggerates, emphasizes, downplays, or otherwise interprets the events that it describes. Most news services emphasise the 'bad' news because they know they will get more viewers that way. Even if they try not to distort reality deliberately, the news media presents things through a very limited lens. They select the descriptive words to use, and the people to interview. They decide which facts deserve emphasis, and how to look at them and interpret them. No matter how compelling and exciting it may seem, the world presented by the mass media is only as real as a passing shadow on the wall of a cave.

You might try to put off your loneliness by going on a shopping spree. The salesman will almost always be nice to you, and your purchases are like gifts to yourself. But the salesman was nice to you not because he liked you, but only because you gave him your money. And when you get home and unwrap the presents you bought for yourself, they will no longer be new. Then you may find yourself empty again, and wanting more.

So you might go shopping for something less materialistic. You might go to "mind, body and spirit" retreat weekends at a "health and wellness" centre. You might seek the services of a therapist or a counselor, a masseur, an aroma-therapist, a yoga instructor, an astrologer or tarot-card reader. You might go to a motivational training weekend, and submit yourself to neuro-linguistic programming, in a huge convention centre with thousands of other people. And you might have paid thousands of dollars to be there. But these are just other forms of market commodities, no less than material goods. They create the illusion of people in your life who care about you. Perhaps some of them do care, but none of them will work for free. (I suspect many of these service providers entered the business in order to surround themselves with needy clients, and thus quell their own loneliness.) Moreover, these solutions almost always simplify the problem too much. They offer gratifying quick-fixes which work only in the short term. When the effect wears off, you have to go back again. Pop psychology solutions can also cost *very* large sums of money, and can economically harm people who need help.

Some people try to escape loneliness by working to gain social prestige or political power. They might do this on a small scale, such as a local church, or a service club, or a neighbourhood residents' organisation. Some aim higher, and run for political offices. If you could surround yourself with supporters, admirers, and followers, then you might have no need to feel any kind of unhappiness. Greed, desire, egotism, and 'self-interest' (the intellectual version of egotism), whether for prestige or wealth or for power, is often explained as the psychological force working within those who climb the corporate ladder, or who strive for high political positions. Some people even experience rushes of pleasure in their ability to shame and humiliate other people. Nonetheless, the acquisition of prestige is not a solution to loneliness. Those who are successful find that success brings only temporary satisfaction. Soon enough, what they have will no longer be enough, and they will desire more. Furthermore, powerful people always have reason to suspect that the others around them are friendly only because they hope to be rewarded for their efforts. The friends and lovers and supporters that one can *buy* are always superficial. And no one can quell the emptiness within him by making himself superior to others. I therefore suspect that even greed itself, one of the most basic of psychological forces, also exists as an unconscious psychological distraction-device against the despair of loneliness.

The relief that these things can provide is always superficial, and always temporary. When it wears off, as it inevitably does, feelings of disappointment and disillusionment can set in. You might go back to them anyway, to try and regain the pleasure and distraction that they can create. But this only perpetuates the problem. Indeed that can create a vicious circle of stimulus and withdrawal which strongly resembles the self-destructive spiral of drug addiction.

§ 3. The Night Watch

Although there is so much loneliness in the world, few people face it directly. Indeed most people will deny feeling any loneliness at all, and they will dismiss all talk of it as too negative and depressing. Perhaps in your mind you have already done this. But I am not concerned here with whether an account of loneliness is 'negative', nor whether it might hurt someone's feelings. I'm concerned with whether it is *true*. Therefore let us face this condition directly, and know it for what it really is.

The kind of loneliness that I wish to address dwells very deeply within us. It is not an accidental circumstance, nor a medical condition, nor a phase in life, nor something which drugs or counseling or 'positive thinking' can cure. Loneliness is an *existential condition*, and a pervasive part of human life.

There is a final occasion of loneliness which cannot be put off or covered up by anything. It appears just as the business of the day has finished itself, and you have no work left to do, and you are lying in bed but not yet asleep. The daily struggle for material security is done, or at least put off to tomorrow. A nightly struggle begins, in which the adversaries are isolation, fear, despair, even boredom. The daily struggle takes place in the world; the nightly struggle, in your mind. That is the moment when loneliness has its chance to find you. A lover might be lying next to you, and you might reach out to her, to stave off loneliness with her companionship. But that will only keep you busy a little while longer. Soon enough one of you will fall asleep, and consign the other to solitude.

Why fear solitude? Some fear it because they fear being unable to reach help if something were to happen: a fall, or a burglar, for instance. Some might have a generalized anxiety disorder. But what of those who don't have such problems to worry about? I suspect that for them, the situation is this. When you are alone, all of your relationships with others are set aside, at least temporarily. In that moment there are no distractions, no escape routes, and no alternatives. All that remains is yourself and – well, yourself alone. Thus to be afraid of loneliness is therefore to be afraid of yourself. To be more clear, perhaps, it is to be afraid of *thinking about who you are*. And the despair of loneliness is the despair that can emerge from such thoughts.

In solitude you must face yourself, without distraction, or denial, or illusion. Many people find that they don't like what they see. Anxieties, shortcomings, failures, bad habits, feelings of shame or guilt, can all rise to the surface, when you are on your own. Some of these feelings are connected to social forces. Marketing campaigns, for instance, constantly tell you that your body is too fat, or that your car isn't fancy and powerful enough, or that your clothes are unfashionable. It tells you that your lifestyle lacks something, whatever it might be. Other things we fear about loneliness are connected to relationships. In solitude you might dwell on the ways in which you have disappointed or hurt people close to you and thus lost some of their love, or gained some of their enmity, or (perhaps worst of all) earned from them a cold-shouldered indifference. Finally, some of these feelings may be more personal, as one becomes conscious of unrequited desires, and unfulfilled dreams. You might fear that you are not good enough, in any number of ways, and that therefore the world will leave you behind.

Most of all, you might fear being *forgotten* by the world. This last fear is perhaps the most subtle and yet the most powerful. Loneliness gives a venue to the thought that *your life might be utterly insignificant and meaningless*, in the grand scheme of things. With nothing and no one to acknowledge your existence, it is easy to imagine that your existence does not deserve that acknowledgment. With nothing and no one to see you and respond to your presence, it is easy to doubt that you exist at all. Loneliness can thus render your life not just insignificant, but *unreal.* For this reason, among others, I describe loneliness as an *existential* condition. And I think it is for this reason, above all others, that most people will do nearly anything at all to avoid loneliness.

The great task of crafting a good and beautiful life cannot properly begin until we honestly recognise the occasions of solitude in our lives. To be is to be alone. Only when this proposition is properly acknowledged can the great work properly begin.

§ 4. The City

Let us ask, as Paul McCartney asked, "All the lonely people: where do they all come from?"

Life in modern, urban, technologically developed, 'Western' societies is such that people often find themselves alienated from each other. We live in such densely populated cities that it is easy to become anonymous, and easy to slide into the banality of 'one more face in the crowd'. I have a friend who, like me, grew up in a small town. She was accustomed to saying hello to strangers, especially to elderly people, who she passed on the street. She learned not to do this when she moved to the 'big smoke' of Toronto. On the third day after settling there, someone she greeted in her usual way followed her home. She had to threaten to call the police to get rid of him. People learn not to make eye contact in big crowds, for fear that the person they greet might be dangerous. Thus for the sake of safety we wear big sunglasses that hide our eyes like masks, and we walk in quick long steps, and we hold our heads up and forward, looking at no one. Nor do we look up or around: one cannot appear to be taking too much interest in the outside world, lest one resemble a tourist, and thus attract pickpockets and thieves. Once we reach home, we draw the curtains, to prevent passer-bys from gawking at our dinner. This serves to isolate people, and to breed loneliness.

It is often the same in the office, the factory, the sales floor, the building site, and the warehouse. Since we spend most of our waking lives at work, it is easy to fall into the belief that our colleagues are our friends. Big companies will sometimes spend enormous amounts of money on team-building workshops and retreats. But one's colleagues are not necessarily one's friends: aside from the shared workplace, we usually have no substantial connection with them. Thus, if the job ever ends, the friendship usually ends too. A Toronto-based human resource consulting company found that someone who discloses too much personal information to colleagues risks damaging his reputation, his professional associations, and may also risk losing his career. (Sarah Boeveld, "I didn't need to know that, sir!" *The Globe and Mail*, 23 February 2009.) Some workplaces have policies which discourage employees from forming emotional or romantic attachments with each other, or even from being too personally friendly. Similarly, we settle in towns and cities surrounded by neighbours with whom we have no necessary connection, aside from a shared property line. These relationships might grow over time and come to be founded on more things than just a job or a city block. Thus they could survive a transfer, a retirement, a move to another town. But this does not refute the transient nature of relationships based solely and entirely on impersonal economic expediency, or the accident of living next door.

Additionally: the more organized and complex a society becomes, the more *division* there is within that society. There will be "butchers, bakers, and candlestick makers": in other words, a system of specialized labour. There will be divisions of property, as when we speak of something as 'yours', and something else as 'mine'. There will be distance between the rich and the poor, and distance between the powerful and the humble. There will be divisions of education, as some finish school and others do not, some go to college or university and others do not. There will be divisions in how one's contribution to society is rewarded, as some people are paid more than others, even when they do the same job. The justice system will separate people into the classes of innocent and guilty, if not into other classes too. There will be differences of political allegiance, which may manifest as your membership in some political party, or your support for some prospective leader. If you express a strong political opinion in a public place, you might be subject to disdainful looks or angry criticisms, which serve to sharpen the distances between you and others.

Let us set aside for the moment any question of whether these divisions are necessary, useful, or natural. Let us simply observe that they emphasise the ways that people are *different* from each other. Therefore they tend to keep people apart, and reinforce the experience of isolation. This loneliness may be especially acute for those who *benefit* from social divisions. The more wealthy and powerful one becomes, the more isolated from others. As Shakespeare wrote, "Uneasy lies the head that wears a crown." Or, as we might say today, "it's lonely at the top."

§ 5. The Individual

Let us also observe that modern societies tend to uphold *individualism* among their most cherished and most frequently affirmed values. Indeed individualism is often taken as a distinctly modern value. Let us define it here as the idea that each person must decide for herself what values will guide her life, and that each person must generate from within herself the purposes she will pursue. She need not refer to anyone else's values to do this, nor does she have to accept any social, political, or cultural sources of value. Indeed individualism supposes that values and purposes are *better*, in the sense of *more worth pursuing*, if they have been generated independently by the free choice of the person who espouses them. It is the generation of value from within, not the nature of the values themselves, which confirms them. Individualism gives a great deal of attention to what philosopher Charles Taylor called 'the culture of authenticity'. This idea has deep roots in the philosophy of Descartes and Locke, and of Romantic philosophy, especially as espoused by people like Rousseau and Herder. Before these figures, the differences between individuals didn't have all that much ethical significance. The culture of authenticity that they created is the idea that each individual has to find his or her own unique way of living life and being human. An authentic person, in this way, is fully 'herself'. Instead of conforming to social models of morality, for instance from religion or from the laws of one's country, one should listen to one's own feelings and intuitions. As Taylor explains it, authenticity is the idea that "there is a certain way of being human that is *my* way. I am called upon to live life in this way, and not in imitation of anyone else's. But this gives a new importance to being true to myself. If I am not, I miss the point of my life, I miss what being human is for *me*." (Taylor, *The Malaise of Modernity*, pg. 29, emphasis his.) This is, indeed, a powerful idea. It has important implications for contemporary political life, for instance in human rights, and the maintenance of a peaceful multiculturalism.

One of the important implications of this ethic of authenticity, however, is that the activity of looking within oneself in this way distances the self from others. The pure-type individualist need not acknowledge the values of her friends and relations. She need not conform to the values of the social groups she happens to be part of, including her family, her religion, even her nationality and culture. If she acknowledges her membership in such groups, this acknowledgement is derived from personal preference alone, and can be withdrawn at any time. It is personal choice that confers meaning on some value; it is not chosen for being already meaningful. Primary education, in most developed western countries, presupposes this point of view. It is designed to turn children into independent adults, able to function on their own, without much need for family support. Similarly, the institution of pension funds presupposes that we expect people to make their own preparations for retirement, and to take care of themselves right to the end of their lives. We don't expect children or grandchildren to take care of their parents and grandparents in their old age, if they don't want to. There may be some support in this world view for qualities like self-reliance and integrity, and a caveat that one's exercise of individual freedom should not interfere with other people's exercise of freedom. There may even be support for the idea that everyone should contribute to society in a meaningful way, although everyone should decide for himself exactly *how* to contribute. But in all cases, she makes her choices by means of her own independent free will.

It follows logically from this situation that all her relationships with other people also emerge only from personal (and changeable) preferences. The individualist enters into marriages, sexual relations, business partnerships, and even ordinary friendships for the sake of her own personal fulfillment, *not* for the sake of the other people involved. Nor does the individualist do this for the sake of 'the relationship' as something that all participants share. Such relationships last only as long as she feels she is getting the most benefit for the least cost. Otherwise, they are interchangeable, and disposable. Any values she may share with others will be a matter of sheer luck that someone else independently chose similar values. It will also be possible to withdraw from such relationships with few consequences. As Taylor explains in several places in his study: "...the dark side of individualism is a centering on the self, which both flattens and narrows our lives, makes them poorer in meaning, and less concerned with others or society." (*ibid*, pg. 4.) With respect to the issue of relationships, he says:

> [Individualism] encourages a purely personal understanding of self-fulfillment, thus making the various associations and communities in which the person enters purely instrumental in their significance. At the broader social level, this is antithetical to any strong commitment to a community. In particular, it makes political citizenship, with its sense of duty and allegiance to political society, more and more marginal. On the more intimate level, it fosters a view of relationships in which these ought to subserve personal fulfillment. (*ibid*. pg. 43.)

I'm fully aware that those who criticise individualism in the smallest way tend to be labeled as socialists (or even as communists), and thus dismissed (if not attacked). But my purpose here is not to dismiss or reject individualism *tout court*. Rather, I am simply drawing attention to a few of its failings. Individualism, in its purest form, simply cannot recognise values that could be shared with others, nor can it recognise values that transcend the individual self. Were it to do so, it would no longer be individualism. To the extent that this is so, individualism separates people, and isolates us from each other. A society of individuals is a society of strangers. This, too, breeds loneliness. Whether this failing outweighs its benefits, I leave for the reader to decide. But let us not measure this failing dishonestly, in an effort to protect what is surely one of the most deeply held, most unquestionable, most fiercely protected, and most 'modern' of our social values.

§ 6. The Man on the Bus

Loneliness also appears on the inter-personal level. I have a friend who described to me a conversation she overheard between an elderly gentleman and a bus driver. The two apparently knew each other, as the man was an occasional rider of that particular route. The man remarked that he was going to a foreign country to visit his daughter, since it was the nine-month anniversary of his wife's death. He also added that he had no other living relations nearby. The bus driver continued talking about road conditions and local news, as if the man had not mentioned his late wife at all. Perhaps the driver felt she had to concentrate on the road. Perhaps she had heard this man complain about his life a hundred times before. But I suspect that even if these practical explanations are true, a deeper problem also obtains here, as I shall now try to explain.

We are often advised that the way to deal with loneliness is to make new friends, or do something to reinvigorate an existing friendship. We are told to 'reach out and touch someone'. This is perhaps the most common kind of solution offered by professional councilors and therapists today. Yet this kind of advice implicitly asks us to search for *someone other than yourself* who, like a kind of Messiah, will descend from a place of unconditional acceptance, and rescue us from our loneliness. But this advice misses an important implication. If the thesis that loneliness is an existential condition is true, it follows that anyone else that a lonely heart might turn to is in exactly the same lonely position. They too are wrapped up in their own isolation. Thus they are almost certainly unable to rescue anyone from loneliness. While one person reaches to another with his plea for help, the person he reaches to is busily pleading with others for help with the same problem. Those others, in their turn, are reaching out to still more others. Almost everyone is looking for someone else to heal their wounds and solve their problems. At the same time, most people will say and do nearly anything to avoid acknowledging someone else's loneliness. Another person's loneliness is too sharp a reflection of one's own, and so people turn away. Those who are not inclined to be self-sacrificing will normally prefer to deal with their own problems. The culture of individualism seems to encourage this: a pure-type individualist always ranks his own interests above those of other people. Most people, therefore, either cannot or will not save someone else from loneliness. More often than not, they will turn their ears away. The true nature and depth of the problem of loneliness is thereby not resolved by reaching out to others. Instead, it is compounded.

§ 7. A Clarification

Let me clarify again that the kind of loneliness which I am describing is not simply a social phenomenon, nor a phase that one passes through, nor a matter of one's attitudes, nor is it a medical condition. Therefore the ways to deal with it which are popularly prescribed today, such as keeping a 'gratitude journal' or reciting positive affirmations, will not help you here. Indeed some recent psychological research has shown that the repetition of self-help mantras doesn't work. The research shows that if the positive affirmation does not match the facts of your life, then you will make yourself feel worse than you already do. ("Self-help makes you feel worse" *BBC News*, online edition, 3rd June 2009.) Nor can this loneliness be quelled by 'breaking out of your comfort zone', or tapping your meridian points to purge negative energy, or whatever new language game the gurus of pop psychology are preaching these days. These ways of understanding loneliness assume that it is 'caused' by something: a loss of innocence, a brain-chemical condition, a frustration of desires, an accumulation of environmental toxins in the body, an excess of unfulfilled expectations and attachments, a failure to manage one's social relations properly, a lack of confidence or initiative, a failure to 'adjust' and 'accept'. Some say that loneliness is merely a product of our social arrangements. It could therefore be reduced by changing whatever social arrangements contribute to it. This is still to assume that loneliness is caused by something, even if that something is social rather than personal.

Part of our loneliness probably can be healed by those ways of dealing with it. Yet there is a dimension of loneliness which is not 'caused' by anything. Rather, it is a property of the nature of things, a mode of the way things are in the world, or to put it simply, *an existential condition of human life.* Consider how loneliness is only tangentially related to how close you are to others. You can feel profoundly connected to someone who is far away; you can feel someone's intimate presence when you are entirely by yourself, in some isolated place. Similarly, you can feel utterly alone in a crowded city, disconnected and alienated from others even as hundreds of others rub shoulders with you in the busy shopping mall. Some people, rather than fearing loneliness, actually crave it. They live and work in social environments where other people constantly make demands upon them. A friend of mine who is the mother of several children told me that being a mother means never being allowed to be alone. Her child is always there, and almost always entirely dependent upon her. Loneliness, or perhaps I should say solitude, is a desirable condition for many people precisely when it is denied to them. My friend said she needs that time to herself, as well as time with adult friends, and without these things she finds herself curiously isolated from herself. All this suggests that loneliness is a very complicated matter, and only tangentially related to the proximity of other people.

Sometimes an idea can be understood better by looking at it from a different culture's perspective. A friend who lives in Brazil described to me a Portuguese word which adds a further dimension of complexity to the matter. The word is *saudade*, which is normally translated into English as 'to miss', as in the saying 'I miss you'. But it is more complex than that:

"You cannot just have saudades of someone. It covers the feeling of missing that which never was, the All and the Nothing, all that no longer is, that could have been, that passed away, those silences that we have lost or no longer see or experience. Because saudade is inherent in us, the fact of being Brazilian and speaking Portuguese forces us to have saudades. And we have them without noticing, and without worrying about the allied feelings: the pain, the sadness, the loneliness, the suffering, the nostalgia." (A. Martins, 2009)

To experience *saudade*, if I understand my friend correctly, is to feel not only loneliness, but also to feel a longing of an existential nature. It is the consciousness of incompleteness, consciousness of the absence of 'the All and the Nothing', and consciousness of isolation because of that absence.

Given all the elements that go into the experience of loneliness, I think it is correct to describe it as a condition of life, an irreducible part of our lived reality. Understood in this way, a person experiencing loneliness is not experiencing a mid-life crisis, nor a momentary lapse of reason, nor is she in the throes of a clinical depression. Rather, she is experiencing one of the deep truths of human existence. This aspect of loneliness cannot be relieved by social change, nor by therapy, nor by antidepressant drugs. It is an Immensity, in a philosophical sense, and even those who think themselves happy are subject to it.

§ 8. The Waterfront

A first part of the existential solitude of human life is the *absolute uniqueness* of every individual person. You have a unique genetic code, unique fingerprints and unique iris patterns. The co-incidence of the time in history and the place on earth where you were born is absolutely distinct. No one will ever be born at the same time and the same place, and with the same genetic code, ever again. The choices you have made over time which took your life in one direction or another, render the biography of your life particularly yours and no other's. These, and a host of other accidents and coincidences, cannot be replicated, not even in theory. There is only one You. There has never been anyone like you ever before in the history of the universe, and there never will be again.

Some see this fact as a reason to think highly of oneself, and feel special and important. However, the facts which make you absolutely unique also apply with equal force to everyone around you. If you are special and important by reason of your absolute uniqueness, it follows that so is everyone else. To explain further: the word 'special' denotes someone who stands out, someone who has peculiarly distinctive qualities. Yet since everyone is equally distinctive, therefore no one stands out. No one possesses any importance above and beyond that which is possessed by others too. The facts which render people unique therefore also, paradoxically, render people equal. Yet this is not the equality of people who have experiences or rights in common. It is the equality of people whose *different* experiences mutually cancel each other out. This kind of equality removes one's reasons for feeling special, without replacing it with common experiences or shared qualities through which one may reach out to others. It therefore tends to sharpen and intensify the isolation people feel.

Since your life is uniquely yours, no one else can get 'inside' it. No one else can see the world from your point of view, except perhaps only partially, incompletely. Each of us has a waterfront: an edge where the circle of one's own being cannot be crossed by another. Beyond that waterfront we can have a shared territory. But we cannot share what is within it, not even in principle. The facts which render you categorically unique in the universe also render others unable to identify with your thoughts, feelings, and purposes, except only tentatively and temporarily. You simply can't see the world from someone else's point of view. Neither can others see the world from yours. However much we give and share of ourselves, and we may give a great deal indeed, one can never give nor share one's absolute uniqueness. However much others may understand your thoughts, or sympathize with your feelings, and they too may understand a great deal, no one will be able to understand you fully, nor sympathize with you completely. There will always be some part of your life that no one else can see. For when others look at your life, they see it through their own eyes, not through yours. And when you look on another person, you see her through your eyes, not hers. To be unique means to be separated from others in this sense. Another person might be able to walk along your waterfront, and see a hilltop on your island, but he cannot climb that hill and view the world from its summit. That view belongs to you alone.

Much of the time people can get along with each other in a practical way anyway, but sometimes this situation becomes a problem. People often assume things about others in order to fill in the gaps of what they don't yet know. They may also have various hopes and expectations about who that person is, which may or may not correspond to the reality. And they might treat that person as if she is who they believe her to be. In this way, elaborate fantasies can be constructed and imposed on others. But reality eventually re-asserts itself. She's not that expected or hoped-for person: she is who *she* is. The illusion is stressed by, and then shattered by, surprising realities that don't fit the fantasy. Some people respond to the shattering of their illusions by looking to hurt that person in return, as if to retaliate for the 'harm' of the shattered fantasy. Thus they spread gossip about that person, or attempt to poison her other friendships. For example, I have a friend whose house was almost sold out from under her by a vindictive and neglectful husband, because she had the audacity to tell him she felt unloved, and to ask him for a divorce.

There will be some who will reject this argument, not because they think it false, but because it attacks the desire to feel special and important. Those who still wish to feel special, who still wish to gain the admiration or even the worship of others, or alternatively their charity and pity, and in either case their *attention*, will have to earn their special status some other way. This will require deeds no one else has done, or possessions and powers that no one else holds. But even this effort is futile: the more powerful, admirable, or special one becomes, the more *set apart* one becomes, and hence the more isolated. To climb to a height is also to climb to a distance.

§ 9. The Distant Shore

Another part of the existential loneliness of human life has to do with the *distance* of other people. No matter how emotionally close you are to another, no matter how familiar you are to each other, there will always be distance between you.

Some of that distance has to do with the uniqueness of people, which I've already described. Yet it may be useful here to explain it further using the concept of 'Otherness'. The idea first appears in the work of Emmanuel Lévinas, an early twentieth century Lithuanian-French philosopher, and has since become enormously influential in ethics, sociology, and psychology. His work is enormously complicated, and to understand it properly it helps to have an understanding of some of his philosophical predecessors, like Husserl, and Heidegger. But it has a very simple core message. Something is Other (with the capital 'O'; from the French *Autrui*) if it is experienced with its independence and identity preserved intact. Ordinary things in the world, when we perceive them, become mixed up in our minds with our expectations, memories, histories, and intentions. We thus enclose them within a common psychological reality; or as Lévinas says, we thus "assimilate them into the Same". But we cannot assimilate other people the same way. They have their own expectations, memories, histories, and intentions. The Other is not simply an opposite of the self, which would imply a hermeneutic relation with the self. Nor is it something which appears as that which is opposed or negated.

The absolutely other is the Other. [*L'absolument Autre, c'est Autrui.*] He and I do not form a number. The collectivity in which I say "you" or "we" is not a plural of the "I". I, you — these are not individuals of a common concept. Neither possession nor the unity of number nor the unity of concepts

31

link me to the Stranger, the Stranger who disturbs the being at home with oneself. But the Stranger also means the free one. Over him I have no power. He escapes my grasp by an essential dimension, even if I have him at my disposal. (Lévinas, *Totality and Infinity*, pg. 39.)

Lévinas' purpose is to rigorously explore the truth that other people are *different* people. The Other has his own presence, his own identity and his own autonomy, different from and independent from my own. If it could be fully known, totally grasped by consciousness or completely enclosed as one's possession, then it would not be Other. The experience of the Other is an encounter that does not lead the observer back to "a point that is always the same". That is, the Other is something which resists being assimilated into one's own perceptual and cognitive activity. Therefore, according to Lévinas, a certain inevitable distance always exists between the self and that which is Other than the self.

Let me add to Lévinas' account of Otherness only this. As long as people are inevitably distant from each other, so they are also lonely. And the occasions in which that distance is brought sharply to attention are the occasions when loneliness holds us the most.

§ 10. The Lovers' Dilemma

Some might say that the obvious solution to the problem of loneliness is love. We hear this teaching all the time, in sources as serious as religious scripture and as superficial as pop music. "Love is a many-splendored thing". "Love lifts us up where we belong". "All you need is love". Most pop songs which mention loneliness do so in the mode of complaint: loneliness is a miserable wasteland, and love is the vehicle of rescue from that wasteland. It sounds very simple, and seems to say all that needs to be said. But love is anything but simple. Love can create numerous frustrations and anxieties in people's lives; it can heighten problems that already exist; it can turn intelligent and good-hearted people into obsessed idiots. We also use the word in reference to many kinds of relationships: brotherly love, filial love, love of one's country, love of boating or hockey, love of God. One might object that love can also motivate people to do great things. It can bring enormous pleasure and meaning to people's lives; it can change people for the better. But these assertions only add strength to the claim that love is something *complicated*. To say that love is the simple solution to loneliness is to probably misunderstand love, and probably to misunderstand loneliness too.

Consider Erich Fromm's famous book *The Art of Loving* (first published in 1956). I choose it because he identifies separateness as the source of our personal and emotional problems. Here are his words:

> The experience of separateness arouses anxiety. It is, indeed, the source of all anxiety. Being separate means being cut off, without any capacity to use my human powers. Hence to be separate means to be helpless, unable to grasp the world – things and people – actively; it means that the world can invade me without my ability to react. Thus, separateness is

the source of intense anxiety. Beyond that, it arouses shame and the feeling of guilt. (Erich Fromm, *The Art of Loving*, pg. 6.)

Fromm's initial idea, that separateness is a source of suffering, is similar to mine. But as you can see in this quote, his account of separateness is rooted in the concept of *power*. Separateness creates anxiety because, according to him, it implies power-lessness: it implies the fear of being invaded and controlled by others. This powerlessness and fear is the source of the anxiety he describes, not loneliness. His definition of love, as the solution to the problem of separateness, is likewise governed by the concept of power. In his words:

...mature love is union under the condition of preserving one's integrity. Love is an active power in man; a power which breaks through the walls which separate man from his fellow men, which unites him with others; love makes him overcome the sense of isolation and separateness, yet it permits him to be himself, to retain his integrity. (*ibid*, pg. 20.)

I understand why Fromm defined love this way. The individualist who loves must preserve his or her initiative and autonomy. If love welled up from the passions without the consent of reason, then the person experiencing love would be in effect controlled by his passions. Like a kind of puppet, he would have lost his freedom. Nonetheless, just as in his description of the problem of separateness, power is the central concept, and love is subordi-nated to the concept of power. But to be fair, this is not the only definition of love that Fromm offers. He also defines it as "active concern for the life and the growth of that which we love." (pg. 25.) Yet even the practical form of this concern, generosity, is described by Fromm as an exercise of will: "Giving is the highest expression of potency. In the very act of giving, I experience my strength, my wealth, my power. This experience of heightened

34

vitality and potency fills me with joy." (pg. 24) This seems to me an almost Nietzschean understanding of generosity: Nietzsche wrote that "The noble human being, too, helps the unfortunate, but not, or almost not, from pity, but prompted more by an urge begotten by excess of power." (Nietzsche, *Beyond Good and Evil*, § 260, pg. 205) And while that understanding of generosity may have much that is admirable about it, nonetheless it presupposes divisions between people, especially *hierarchical* divisions based on power, in which one party has the power to give, and the other does not and thus merely receives. Yet surely the point of love is to foster *closeness!* With perhaps very few exceptions, if any at all, a categorical disjunction exists between the expression of love and the exercise of power. You can love something, and selflessly care for it, *or* you can impose your will on it. You cannot do both at the same time. Thus I suspect this notion of love cannot quell loneliness. Indeed I suspect it does little to help promote a flourishing life either.

Anyone who truly, deeply, and honestly loves someone knows that love is not the exercise of power over the beloved. In fact love is often experienced as a *loss* of power. Consider, for example, *The Grief of a Young Girl's Heart*, which I consider one of the finest love poems ever composed. Part of it reads as follows:

When I go by myself to the Well of Loneliness, I sit down and I go through my trouble; when I see the world and do not see my boy, he that has an amber shade in his hair.

It was on that Sunday I gave my love to you; the Sunday that is last before Easter Sunday. And myself on my knees reading the Passion; and my two eyes giving love to you for ever.

O, aya! my mother, give myself to him; and give him all that you have in the world; get out yourself to ask for alms, and do not come back and forward looking for me.

35

My mother said to me not to be talking with you to-day, or to-morrow, or on the Sunday; it was a bad time she took for telling me that; it was shutting the door after the house was robbed...

You have taken the east from me; you have taken the west from me; you have taken what is before me and what is behind me; you have taken the moon, you have taken the sun from me; and my fear is great that you have taken God from me!

(from Lady Gregory, ed. *The Kiltartan Poetry Book*, pg. 24-26.)

This exquisite poem originates in the oral culture of Ireland's west province. Indigenous Irish language and culture was still strong in that area at the time that Lady Gregory translated and published this piece. It must be read aloud for its fullest impact to be perceived (and I recommend the recitation that appears in John Huston's 1987 film, *The Dead.*) It expresses, among other things, the way that love sometimes worsens the feeling of separateness, rather than heals it. Love can render life *more* frustrating, *more* painful. Some parts of the poem, like the demands the speaker makes on her mother, and her inability to concentrate during the Mass, suggest that she has not preserved but actually *lost* her sense of self. Furthermore she describes her experience of love precisely as the kind of invasion that Fromm says causes anxiety. This is particularly evident in the artistically powerful last lines of the piece.

Love, at least when connected to power, is not the answer to the problem of loneliness. But I have not said the last word about love here. Love does indeed have an important place in the spiritual life. But I shall have to put off the full account of that place until later.

§ 11. The Solitude of God

Some might believe that loneliness can be lessened or overcome by some kind of religious activity. You might therefore learn meditation, start praying more often, go on a spiritual retreat or a pilgrimage, make various confessions of faith, or involve yourself in charitable work or other similar activities. You might practice a more private kind of religion, seeking divine knowledge by means of direct personal experience, or by some kind of 'one-ness' with the universe. Yet I think this, too, is no escape. The very process of achieving spiritual wholeness with the world, with 'the One' or 'the All' (or whatever), is in its essence a systematic assimilation of others into the circle of one's own being. The mystic who feels at one with the world finds only himself there – he finds no true others. The more at one you feel with the world, the fewer 'others' there are. Thus the more isolated and alone one becomes.

Consider, for instance, the dialogue in the *Bhagavad Gita* between a soldier named Arjuna, and the Hindu god Krishna. In part of the dialogue, Krishna says:

He whose self is harmonized by *yoga* sees the Self abiding in all beings and all beings in the Self; everywhere he sees the same.

He who sees Me everywhere and sees all in Me – I am not lost to him nor is he lost to Me.

The *yogin* who, established in oneness, worships Me abiding in all beings lives in Me, howsoever he may be active.

He, O Arjuna, who sees with equality everything, in the image of his own self, whether in pleasure or in pain – he is considered a perfect *yogi*.

(*Bhagavad Gita*, 6:29-32)

This passage is often quoted by spiritual people both east and west as a statement of comprehensive spiritual wholeness. It describes spiritual practice as the systematic elimination of the distance between yourself and all other people and things in the world. The *yogi*, the spiritual practitioner, is encouraged to see everything in his perceptual experience as a part of himself, and himself as part of all things. He is also to see all things as part of the divine body of the god Krishna, in whom he dwells, and who dwells within him. This is an interesting thought, frequently quoted not only for its spiritual intrigue, but also for its social and political implications. It expresses the idea that suffering and oppression is rooted in our *differences*, be they differences of sex, race, culture, nationality, religion, or social class. A world of total one-ness would be a world without differences, a word without 'others', and thus a world without conflict and competition with others, and thus a world of peace. After all, if you see yourself everywhere, then conflict and warfare would appear rather pointless. You would only be fighting yourself.

Nonetheless, these lines teach a veritable formulae for loneliness. Its thesis is that only one conscious and self-aware person exists in the whole of the universe (that is, God). If this thesis is true, however, then that singular person must find himself isolated in the universe in an *absolute* sense. If my general thesis is correct, and loneliness is indeed an existential condition, then not even God can save us. He, too, is in exactly the same position as the man on the bus.

Here's the reason why. Another part of the loneliness of human life has to do with the *absolute solitude of the universe as a whole*. The totality of the universe is a wide vista of space, an almost unimaginable vastness of space. We see that it is full of planets, asteroids, comets, nebulae, stars, clusters of stars, galaxies, clusters of galaxies. Yet there are unimaginably vast reaches of absolutely empty space between them. The planet on which we live is but one infinitesimally small pinprick of warmth moving through a vast bottomless sea, in which the very notion of warmth has no meaning. This, too, is a source of loneliness. Where we mere mortals might imagine or mathematically calculate the distance between the stars, the gods probably feel that distance right in their bones. If we imagine that the greatness of a god is her immanent presence in and with all things, or his transcendental presence through and beyond all things, then surely a god is *even more lonely* than a humble human being. For a god would know better than mere mortals the emptiness between the planets, and the silence between the stars.

Yet the true loneliness of the universe is not just its vast empty spaces. The loneliness of the universe is also the fact that the universe, considered as a totality, has nothing other than itself. There is no 'other' for the universe as a whole to relate to: it has no 'outside'. There is no possibility for companionship for the universe as a whole. (Some mathematicians think there might be multiple universes. In that case, we would be living in a complex 'multiverse' which, again, has nothing outside of itself.)

Thus the universe is alone in an absolute sense. The gods, if they exist, and if they are some of the things people believe about them, are in a much better position to understand this loneliness than you and I. And they probably ache with that knowledge far worse than you and I. Therefore they, too, need to reach out to others; they too seek companionship. One of my favourite passages from the Upanisads suggests that God created the universe precisely to quell his own loneliness:

In the beginning this world was Self (Atman) alone in the form of a Person. Looking around, he saw nothing else than himself. He said first, "I Am". Thence arose the name "I"...

He was afraid, for one who is alone is afraid. This one said to himself, "Since there is nothing else than myself, of what am I afraid?" Thereupon, truly, his fear departed, for of what should he have been afraid? Assuredly it is from a second that fear arises.

Verily, he had no delight, for one who is alone has no delight. He was, indeed, as large as a woman and a man closely embraced. He caused that self to fall into two pieces. Therefore this is true: "Oneself is like a half-fragment"...

He copulated with her. There from human beings were produced.

(*Brhadaranyaka Upanisad* I.iv.1-5)

Notice that God's first spoken word in this account was an assertion of presence: "I am". We'll see more of that later on.

From here the text describes how the Atman and his partner changed themselves into the forms of various animals, and copulated again to create all the different animal species. The Atman did this in order to populate the universe, to bring *others* into being. These others are part of himself, as they came from himself. Yet they are also different from himself – they are estranged from the whole. Precisely because of that estrangement, they can potentially fulfill a need that God cannot fulfill on his own: a need to relate to others.

§ 12. The Wisdom of Lucretius

The solitude of God, and the absolute solitude of the universe as a whole, is perhaps not obviously apparent in most people's ordinary lives. Yet there are occasions in every person's life in which the absolute loneliness of the universe intervenes itself. Foremost among them is Death. The passing of a friend, a family member, or a beloved companion, or even a public figure that you happen to admire, is the kind of change in one's life that leaves feelings of profound emptiness and loss. The death of someone who had formed a part of the circle of your transpersonal existence compels your attention to the incompleteness of one's own life, and draws attention to the fragility of one's life and one's relationships.

Some might seek comfort in the thought that since everyone must die, everyone has at least that in common. But consider a favourite saying of the ancient Greek philosopher Lucretius: "While one lives one does not die; when one dies there is no one there for death to claim; thus death never reaches you." The implication that Lucretius wants us to find in this argument is that no one need fear death. Some two thousand years later Ludwig Wittgenstein, the great scholar of logic, reached a similar conclusion: "Death is not an experience of life; we do not live to experience death." (*Tractatus Logico-Philosophicus*, 6.4311) The soundness of the argument depends on a trick in the logic of language. To say 'I shall die' is to treat death like a real event in the world. But death is not an event in the world: it is actually the *cessation* of an event in the world. Death is a non-event that no one experiences. Nonetheless, it is still true that life is an event with an expiry date. No amount of logical hair-splitting can change that brute fact.

There is another thing which this argument shows, and which apparently neither Lucretius nor Wittgenstein mentioned. Since death is not an event in life, therefore it also cannot be held in common with others. Since death is a non-event that no one experiences, therefore it cannot be shared. There is thus no question of passing the experience on to anyone else, for him to endure on your behalf. No one dies 'for' another. Nor is there any enduring it with others at your side, nor comparing notes with others who have had similar experiences. Your death-bed might be in a hospice, surrounded by numerous people: your doctor and a few nurses, members of your family, and the most intimate of your friends. But these people are not sharing your experience. They are having their own experience of your passing. You might believe in out-of-body experiences, near-death experiences, or in the capacity of souls to survive death and maybe even contact the living. But none of these beliefs refute the basic truth that your death is inherently non-transferable. Whatever else may happen, you will die alone.

These existential reasons why life is lonely cannot be rectified by a change in the social order. They are an inherent part of how we exist in the world. So long as we are alive, there is no escape from the occasional yet persistent reminder that each person is a world unto herself, living at an acute distance from others, even those nearest to her. This loneliness inserts itself into our lives even to the very end. Loneliness is an Immensity.

§ 13. The Great Silence

This discussion of loneliness may strike many readers as upsetting. But I would surely be a bad philosopher if I rejected some idea for no other reason than because I thought my friends might dislike it! Take note, however, that I present this case not as a conclusion that must be graciously or grudgingly accepted. Recognition of the facts of the case does not have to lead to resignation and surrender. I present the case as a *problem that must be solved*. I am certain that this is a *real* problem, and that it affects a great many people. I am also certain that solutions exist.

I have a friend who lived for a year alone in a trailer in northern Alberta, Canada. In the summer, she found the solitude welcoming. She described to me how she quickly became attuned to the environment, for instance by waking and sleeping with the sun. She would leave the window open at night to hear the wind and rain, and then "drift off to sleep contentedly knowing I am safe... glad to be alone with my bed, my dog and the land." But she described her experience of solitude in the winter very differently:

"There is no rustle of leaves, no gentle rushing of the wind through trees, no tinkle from the now frozen streambed. No birds sing, no animal pass by. Even the coyotes are tucked away somewhere, hiding from the cold. The silence of snow falling on a northern landscape is deafening. The cold and the silence make my solitude that much more acute." (J. Cox, 2009)

I've a few occasions in my life which are a lot like the one she described here, and I'm sure you do too. But although I think loneliness is a problem, I do not think it is evil. Loneliness can be hard, and can induce strong feelings of melancholy, worthlessness, fear, and sometimes even madness. But it is not like a disease, for which we should be looking for a cure. Nor is it a kind of oppression, against which we should be staging some kind of rebellion. Loneliness is a condition of existence. It is just part of the way things are. My friend's letter here shows that loneliness can be experienced in many ways by the same person. While it may not always be a happy condition, there may be ways to learn to live with it, and there may be ways to benefit from it.

Many important philosophers and artists, for instance, found that they needed solitude and quiet in order to have their own thoughts. Beethoven used to walk in the countryside around Vienna for hours every day. Some of his most recognisable melodies, such as the famous first four notes of the Fifth Symphony, were based on the sounds of bird calls and the other natural sounds. Jean Jacques Rousseau developed his philosophical ideas while walking alone across the Swiss Alps. Boethius wrote his famous *Consolation of Philosophy*, one of the most influential philosophical books of the whole middle ages, while he was in solitary confinement in a prison in Ravenna.

In much of the world's religious literature, for instance, solitude and privacy and silence are necessary parts of the story of how a religious hero gained his divine revelation. The enlightenment of Siddhartha Gautama, the first Buddha, occurred when he was alone in the forest, beneath the Bodhi tree, at the moment of sunrise. Moses had to climb the slopes of Mount Sinai, alone, to speak with God and receive the Ten Commandments. Jesus achieved his spiritual victory over evil after he had wandered in the desert alone for forty days. Similarly, his 'passion' in the garden of Gethsemane, when the loneliness of humanity overwhelmed him, was endured alone, for earlier that evening he had left his apostles behind. Subsequent Christian saints like Theresa of Avila, Julian of Norwich, and Francis of Assisi, received their divine revelations in the quiet privacy of their monastery cells, or while walking in forests and natural settings alone. The revelation of Mohammed, peace be upon him, similarly occurred in solitude. In his middle age he was in the habit of giving a few weeks of every year to quiet meditation in a cave on Mount Hira, near Mecca. On one of those occasions, when he was about 40 years old, the angel Gabriel visited him and dictated to him the words that would eventually become the Koran.

These examples come from the 'great' religions of the world. But the seeking of spiritual revelation in solitude happens in minority traditions too. Think of the Norse god Odin who hung himself from the World Tree for nine days in order to gain the knowledge of how to read and write the runes (that is, the knowledge of knowledge itself). Druids, the mystics and philosophers of the ancient Celtic people, constructed their sacred places in hidden sanctuaries in forests. The Roman poet Lucan said of them, "the innermost groves of far-off forests are your abodes." (Lucan, *Pharsalia*, I.453). Other sources describe how Druids also sought caves, hilltops, islands, and other isolated places, particularly if the landscape was rugged and the weather was harsh. This tradition continued after the arrival of Christianity: some of the Celtic world's most important centres of Christian culture were on remote islands like Iona, Lindisfarne, and Skellig Michael. Early Irish Christian monks would sometimes go into isolation for many years, seeking God on hilltops and remote islands. They called this kind of solitary seeking "White Martyrdom".

Aboriginal people in North America have a tradition in which young people must seek out loneliness, as a rite of passage into adulthood. This tradition is popularly called the Vision Quest, although it has many names. The vision quest requires a young person who is ready to enter adulthood to go away from his home, and find an isolated place some distance away, perhaps several day's walk away. He might be provisioned with some equipment, and food, but for the most part he has to survive on his own. Yet the vision quest is not a test of his survival skills. It is a test of his mind. He has to be able to survive on his own without losing his sanity. He also has to be able to find, in his dreams or his thoughts or in some special perception, a communication from the Great Spirit. It might be the knowledge of which animal is his special guardian. It might be a 'power song' which in the future he can sing whenever about to go hunting. The point, however, is that it is communicated to him especially in his solitude. He will have to live at that place, for however long it takes, until he receives his communication. It can take many days, even weeks. Some people return from their vision quests after years. It's worth adding that many Aboriginal cultures around the world have some variation of this tradition. Among Aboriginal people of Australia, for instance, the custom is called a Walkabout.

Consider as a final example the following story described by Roald Amundsen, one of the first Europeans to explore the North West Passage. One year he decided to spend the winter among the Inuit people, instead of going home, and he shared a living space with a shaman. He observed that the shaman used sleight-of-hand tricks to create the illusion of performing works of magic for his clients. Amundsen asked if the shaman was ever troubled by the fact that he was deceiving the people who sought his help. The shaman smiled and replied:

My magic power is not in my tricks. My real power is that I have gone out on the ice and lived there alone for many months until I could finally hear the voice of the Universe. And the voice of the Universe is that of a mother calling after her beloved children. That is my real magic.

(Hamilton & Weil, *The Scalpel and the Soul*, from the introduction by Sir James Jeans pg. xii.)

In the case of the Inuit shaman's 'real magic', as in every case of the reception or discovery of divine wisdom, there is a withdrawal from the world. The mystic retreats from the dramatic noise of society, and enters the equally dramatic silence of a private and entirely spiritual realm.

The idea of spiritual knowledge discovered in solitude and silence is a prominent part of many ancient spiritual cultures. I think this is because ancient people discovered something in it which is powerful. Without other people to deal with, relate to, or be distracted by, you can attend to the world as a comprehensive whole, and to your own interior world. Perhaps the voice of the universe, which the Inuit shaman spoke of, is always calling out to us, but we hear it only in the rare moments when all distractions have been put aside. It is perhaps for this reason that one of the Old Testament prophets speaks of the necessity to observe the presence of God in silence: "Yahweh is in his holy temple, let all the earth keep silence before him." (Habacuc 2:20) Rudolph Otto, in his landmark book *The Idea of the Holy* (first published 1923) wrote that silence is one of the ways in which we approach the sacred. It is not, he says, that one fears accidentally uttering "words of evil omen", and therefore refrains from speaking. Rather, he says that silence is "a spontaneous reaction to the feeling of the actual *numen prasens*." (Otto, *The Idea of the Holy*, pg. 68-9.) What I think he means by this is that when in the presence of the numinous, we respond with silence, so that the numinous will not be interrupted.

What Otto says about silence, I think applies to solitude as well. For silence is a form of solitude: in the absence of other people's speaking voices around you, your world becomes entirely your own. Silence can breed loneliness too: for there are no other voices to acknowledge your own. Yet from this silent solitude, powerful experiences can emerge. Think of the silence between you and your lover as you hold each other at night. Perhaps something stressful or upsetting happened to one of you, and the other offers a shoulder to lean on. It is similar, I think, when one sits on a hilltop, gazing upon the earth below and the sky above, without any plans of action but to attend to the beauty of what you see. An awareness of the here-ness and the now-ness of being, uncomplicated and unqualified by any lesser concerns, can arise here. Silence is peaceful in an absolute sense. This awareness can fill you with a sense of loneliness, solitude, and sometimes of insignificance. But it can also create a sense of wonder, welcome, and belonging. The solitude of silence is a condition of pure and perfect peace. This, I think, is the important spiritual knowledge which only solitude can bring.

§ 14. The Towers

A question appeared in my mind as I contemplated the Inukshuks of northern Canada, and the portal dolmen of western Ireland. Might both of them have been built as a response to loneliness? Yet this prospect also led me to further questions. How could *buildings* help us deal with loneliness? And what about other forms of public art? As I contemplated these questions, they soon appeared to be about not just history and archaeology. They also became questions about human life in general, including matters of personal, social, and political values in technologically advanced modern societies. I began to see a common revelation in all kinds of public monuments in every city I had recently visited: the Old Town Clock in Halifax, Nova Scotia, the oldest of its kind on the continent of North America; The CN Tower in Toronto, with its colourful light display; the rotating beacon that shines from the top of Place Ville-Marie in Montreal; the Chateau Frontenac, in Quebec City; the Bastille in Grenoble, France. These buildings were constructed primarily for utilitarian reasons. The Clock Tower in Halifax is a civic timekeeper from the days before people had kitchen clocks and wrist watches. The C.N. Tower is a radio and television broadcast pylon. Place Ville-Marie is an office block and shopping centre. The Chateau Frontenac is a hotel. And the Bastille of Grenoble was once a military fortification, and is now an open-air museum. Some monuments I visited were built not for utilitarian purposes but instead for aesthetic, cultural, or religious reasons. The Elizabethenkirshen, in Marburg Germany, is a Lutheran cathedral, and like many religious buildings it was designed to glorify God. The Long Man of Wilmington, in the South Downs of Sussex, England, is a huge outline figure of a man (but it could be a woman) carved into a hillside. Its age and original purpose is sufficiently mysterious that it can mean just about anything you want it to mean. Above Lake Como, in northern Italy, a lighthouse beams out the colours of the Italian flag: green, white, and red. Lake Como is not so large that it really needs a lighthouse, but having one there contributes to the town of Como's identity, and lends to that identity a touch of fun. Lloyd's Tower, near the town of Kells, Ireland, is another almost-useless lighthouse, since it stands sixty kilometers inland. A local landlord in the nineteenth century built it to commemorate his sons, who lost their lives at sea. The Millennium Spire, in Dublin, is a two hundred meter steel spike in the centre of Ireland's most historically significant city street. It tapers from two meters wide at the base to ten centimeters at the top, so a person standing next to it would think it stands a million miles high. This optical illusion was particularly effective for me on clear starry nights. It was built to celebrate the continuity of Irish culture from prehistory to the present, although many believe it was built to celebrate a certain politician's ego. These monuments serve as practical demonstrations of the technological power and political will of the society that built them. They also attract tourists. But otherwise, they were built for non-commercial, non-military, and generally non-utilitarian reasons.

Somewhere in the fall of 2008, just after I visited the Long Man, all these places began to remind me of the Neolithic stone monuments of the west of Ireland, and the Inukshuks of the Canadian Arctic. I began to suspect that another reason lurked behind the cultural and practical purposes of these buildings, and other great world monuments too. The Pyramids of Giza, the Eiffel Tower in Paris, the statue of Christ Redeemer in Rio de Janeiro, the Hagia Sophia in Istanbul, and the Forbidden City of Beijing, might be *in principle* fulfilling the same existential need in the human spirit as a modest Canadian Inukshuk, or a humble Irish Neolithic tomb. Perhaps they were built not only for the obvious economic or practical purposes, but also to establish a visible human presence in the world. Perhaps they, too, demonstrate that the world is a populated world, and thus they serve to make the world less lonely.

§ 15. The Concert

Imagine yourself settling into your seat at a concert, just before your favourite musician takes the stage. It might be a local garage band trying to get started, and perhaps the members of the band are friends of yours. It might be a world-famous pop singer, performing before thousands of people in a football stadium. It might be a kitchen racket, an informal gathering of musicians and friends in a private home. For my part, I'm in a park in a small town, where ornate lamp posts light the way through a grove of old maples and oaks to the hillside amphitheatre. My friend and I are going to hear a performance of Beethoven's Ninth Symphony. I've smuggled in a bottle of Pinot Noir, and my friend brought a blanket to spread on the grass. There is polite applause when the performers take the stage – perhaps in the pub people shout and whistle, perhaps in the stadium people scream – and then there is a moment of silence, just before the performance begins.

It's the silence just before the performance that interests me (which perhaps those in the stadium never hear). Some people may perceive the silence as full of possibility and potential. A kind of elastic tension can be felt, compelling the mind forward in time. In silence we anticipate the performance to come. Anything may happen next, and so we feel excited. But to emphasise that anticipation, as a quality of the silence, is to claim that silence is *something*, and thus to miss the point. The silence itself is not full of potential and possibility. It is precisely *empty* of such things, since precisely nothing is happening. Silence is not music; silence is not potential sound. *Silence is nothing*. Silence is not a different kind of presence, like a different kind of sound. It is the *absence* of sound. It is the absence of presence, and the presence of absence. Actually, to say such things about silence is to fall into contradictions of language, for the sentence treats 'nothing' as if it is a 'something' which silence can 'be'. Such is the insidiousness of language when 'nothingness' is involved. But I trust the point is clear. Those who would emphasise the anticipation in the silence are actually missing the silence. If you attend to the silence itself, you remain in the present moment without imposing anticipations upon it. In that moment, you can hear the emptiness of the cold arctic plain, or the windy Irish field, where no cairn yet stands.

A voice cries out in the desert: make way for the musician! The performance has begun. Now, on the hillside where my friend rolls out her blanket and I pour out my smuggled wine, there is silence no longer. There is an opera, or a symphony, or a choral performance, or just the formality of applauding the conductor as he enters. At the pub there is the tuning of guitars and the testing of microphones. At the stadium there are the screams of the fans. But most of all, there is *something rather than nothing*. The singer that quells the silence with her voice is like the Inukshuk that quells the isolation of the arctic plain, and the portal dolmen that quells the solitude of the Burren. Each in their own peculiar way pushes back the silence; each asserts the presence of something-that-is-not-nothing; each holds the loneliness of the world at bay for a while.

§ 16. The Ripples on the Water

In his *Introductory Lectures on Aesthetics*, the German philosopher G.W.F. Hegel asked the question: "What is man's need to produce works of art?" His answer is expressed in the following parable.

A boy throws stones into the river, and then stands admiring the circles that trace themselves on the water, as an effect in which he attains the sight of something that is his own doing. This need traverses the most manifold phenomena, up to the mode of self-production in the medium of external things as it is known to us in the work of art. And it is not only external things that man treats in this way, but himself no less, i.e. his own natural form, which he does not leave as he finds it, but alters of set purpose... (Hegel, *Phenomenology of Spirit*, pg. 36)

The idea here is that people create art in order to fulfill a need to render the world recognisable, intelligible, and our own. We create art in order to see ourselves, as if from outside, and thus to recognise and to know ourselves. I see in this parable an instance of the idea that the implicit purpose of art, including music and architecture, is to assert presence, and thus render the world less lonely. Hegel's way of saying this is: "The universal need for expression in art lies, therefore, in man's rational impulse to exalt the inner and outer world into a spiritual consciousness for himself, as an object in which he recognises his own self." (*ibid.* pg. 36). But a much simpler and more obvious way to say what amounts to the same thing is this: The boy drops his pebbles into the water in order to assert to himself, and anyone else who may be watching, 'I am here!'

Premonitions of Nietzsche can be discerned here. Less than a hundred years after Hegel, Nietzsche published *The Birth of Tragedy: Out of the Spirit of Music*. On the first page he described art as "the metaphysical activity of man". What might that mean? Here's a passage from an early chapter of the text which I think helps to explain it.

> Amongst the Greeks the 'will' wished to contemplate itself, in the transfiguration of genius and the world of art; in order to glorify themselves, its creations had to feel worthy of glorification. They had to see themselves in a higher sphere, without this contemplation seeming either a command or a reproach. It was in this sphere of beauty that they saw reflections of themselves, the Olympians. (Nietzsche, *The Birth of Tragedy*, pg. 24)

People create art, especially mythology (as a form of art), because they want to see themselves as *real*. Not only that, but we want to see ourselves in a better, higher, more divine light– not just as we are, but also as we wish ourselves to be. For this reason, Nietzsche seems to say, we use art and mythology to inscribe ourselves on to the structure of the universe.

In a subsequent text, *Beyond Good and Evil*, Nietzsche explains himself further by asking the question, why do people pray? Surely not to God, for Nietzsche believed that God is dead and so there is no question of a supernatural being making its presence known to us. The devout believer at prayer is therefore caught up in a massive case of self-delusion. Or, he is doing something a little more subtle: he is giving honour to a representation of human power and greatness. In his words:

> So far the most powerful human beings have still bowed worshipfully before the saint as the riddle of self-conquest and deliberate final renunciation. Why did they bow? In him—and as it were behind the question mark of his fragile and miserable appearance—they sensed the superior force that sought to test itself in such a conquest, the strength of the

will in which they recognised and honoured their own strength and delight in dominion: they honoured something in themselves when they honoured the saint. (Nietzsche, *Beyond Good and Evil*, §51, pg. 65)

This, I think, is Nietzsche's way of continuing the Hegelian metaphor of the ripples on the water. We create art, and indeed mythology and religion and civilisation, in order to see ourselves and know that we exist. And moreover, we want to see ourselves not just anywhere, but on the highest plane, 'exalted into a spiritual consciousness'.

Neither Hegel nor Nietzsche mention loneliness here. Yet it may have an unacknowledged place in both accounts. Perhaps the human being needs to see the effect of his labour on the world because that would be a sign of a human presence, even if only his own. That sign of a human presence is the expression of an 'I am here!' which gives him some company. We populate the world with heroes, gods, saints, and spirits, because we cannot face the prospect of an empty and unpopulated world. We make them like ourselves so that we will be able to recognise them, identify with them, and glorify ourselves through them. But most importantly, we want to call out to the world, and cannot bear the thought that no one will ever hear us, nor will anyone ever reply.

§ 17. "I am Here!"

Any kind of artistic creativity also implies a hidden underlying *assertion of presence*. It might be a hand-made stone circle in the midlands of Ireland, or a pair of concrete and steel office buildings in modern Singapore. It might be a kitchen racket in a Newfoundland fisherman's house or an opera by Puccini in the Coliseum of Rome. By 'presence' here, I mean the here-ness and now-ness of something-that-is-not-nothing. One who asserts her presence this way asserts that she *exists*, and that her existence *matters*. Although the assertion of presence resists being cast into words, it takes the form of a greeting, an announcement, a calling-out to the world: it says '*I am here!*'. Whatever other message is being offered, this assertion of the here-ness and the now-ness of she who speaks, must also appear. This is a phenomenological necessity. A song implies a singer; a building implies a builder; a message implies a messenger; a speech implies a speaker. In each case, whatever else the message may be, there is also the implicit message of the presence of the speaker. That implicit message has the logical structure of the statement 'I am here!'

This implicit logical expression is an existential assertion of presence. But perhaps it would also be correct to call it the Revelation.

I use the word 'revelation' to suggest something theological. It is, after all, the name of the final book of the Christian Bible. But I wish to use it in the simpler sense of its root verb 'to reveal'. A Revelation, as I shall understand the word in this study, is an event or an occasion in which *something of existential and spiritual significance appears*. This could be a visionary experience of God, with all the strange symbols and epic drama of the biblical fable. Yet I think it no less spiritually significant when it is a revelation of another human being, however simple and humble he may be.

In its most elemental meaning, a Revelation is an experience of the presence of any being capable of asserting its own existence in the world as a first-order proposition.

Consider as another example, the early Irish legend of the arrival of the Milesian tribe on Ireland, which is really the story of the arrival of the human race on Earth. When the Milesians arrive, the ruling tribe at the time, the Tuatha de Dannan, tell the Milesian leaders they can settle on Ireland if they retreat in their ships as far from the shore as 'the ninth wave' (meaning the horizon). Then if they can make landfall again, they can settle in Ireland permanently. When the Milesians do this, the Tuatha de Dannan create a magical sea storm to ward them away. The chief poet and druid of the Milesian tribe, Amergin, climbs to the top of the mast and recites a magical poem which calms the storm. When the ships make landfall, Amergin is then the first of his tribe to set foot on the shore. He then speaks another magical poem which is now sometimes called *The Mystery*, and sometimes called after its author the *Song of Amergin*. Here is one version of it.

I am the wind on the sea;
I am the wave of the sea;
I am the bull of seven battles;
I am the eagle on the rock;
I am the flash from the sun;
I am the most beautiful of plants;
I am a strong wild boar;
I am a salmon in the water;
I am a lake in the plain;
I am the word of knowledge;
I am the head of the spear in battle;
I am the god that puts fire in the head;
Who spreads light in the gathering on the hills?
Who can tell the ages of the moon?

Who can tell the place where the sun rests?
(Lady Gregory, *Gods and Fighting Men*, pg. 74)

Here the logical form of the Revelation is stated almost explicitly. Amergin lists a variety of things and events that are symbolically and magically significant in his culture. For instance, 'the salmon in the water' probably refers to the Salmon of Knowledge, the one animal in Celtic mythology which is able to reach and return from the Well of Wisdom. The 'flash from the sun' probably refers to the Neolithic passage mound, built to permit direct sunlight to pass from the gate to the back wall of the central chamber on only one day of the year. Yet Amergin says that he *is* that salmon, and he *is* that sunbeam. In each line of the poem, Amergin asserts that his presence comprehensively reveals itself in each of these mythological creatures and places. It is as if the landscape itself was asserting its own presence through the words of the poet. It says 'I am here!', through Amergin, in twelve different ways.

In the context of the story, Amergin is also proudly boasting that he and his tribe landed their ships on Ireland despite the resistance raised against them. In other words, he says 'I and my tribe are *here*, in Ireland; I defeated you, I'm the greatest!' (Imagine this poem recited by Mohammed Ali, just after winning a title match). Yet I think it significant that this boast was made in the form of a declaration of comprehensive spiritual presence. Amergin was able to land on Ireland because he identified himself with Ireland. He put himself into a frame of mind in which he was able to look upon the landscape of Ireland, its animals, its rivers, its trees, and say to himself 'I am.' Each line of the poem is another way of saying 'I belong here, in this place; I recognise in these things my values, my identity, my very selfhood; being here is how I know who I am.' And each of these statements is, again, a different way of saying 'I am here!'

Consider also the following similar passage from the

59

Bhagavad Gita, which also has an instance of the assertion of presence:

There is nothing that is higher than I, O Winner of Wealth (Arjuna). All that is here is strung on me as rows of gems on a string.

I am the taste in the waters, O Son of Kunti (Arjuna). I am the light in the moon and sun. I am the syllable Aum in all the Vedas. I am the sound in ether and manhood in men.

I am the pure fragrance in earth and brightness in fire. I am the life in all existences and the austerity in ascetics.

Know me, O Partha, to be the eternal seed of all existences. I am the intelligence of the intelligent. I am the splendor of the splendid.

I am the strength of the strong, devoid of desire and passion. In beings I am the desire which is not contrary to law (*dharma*), O Lord of the Bharats.

And whatever states of being there may be, be they harmonious, passionate, slothful—know thou that they are all from Me alone. I am not in them; they are in Me.

(*Bhagavad Gita* 7:7-12.)

Krishna of course is a god, not a human being, and so it is easier to interpret His statement in a theological kind of way. His words assert that everything in the world is part of His divine presence. The waters of a river, the sun and moon, the beauty of beautiful things, are all different ways that Krishna reveals himself to humanity. Nor is this the only passage of this kind in the text. (For instance, the pattern appears again at 9:16-19 and 10:19-38.)

Here's a third example, from the story of *The Golden Ass*. This was a comic novel, written some time in the late Roman empire, about a man named Lucius Apuelius who was magically transformed into a donkey. Near the end of the story, Lucius prays to the goddess Isis to be restored to his normal human form. Then he fell asleep. In his dream the goddess appeared to him and said:

You see me here, Lucius, moved by your prayer. I am Nature, the universal Mother, mistress of all the elements, primordial child of time, sovereign of all things spiritual, Queen of the Dead, first also among the immortals, the single manifestation of all gods and goddesses there are. My nod governs the shining heights of Heaven, the wholesome sea-breezes, the lamentable silences of the world below. Though I am worshipped in many aspects, known by countless names and propitiated with all manner of different rites, yet the whole earth venerates me. The primeval Phrygians call me the Goddess of Pessinus, Mother of the Gods; the Athenians, sprung from their own soil, call me the Minerva of Cecrops' citadel; for the islanders of Cyprus I am Paphian Venus; for the archers of Crete I am Diana Dictynna; for the trilingual Sicilians, Stygian Proserpine; and for the Eleusinians, their ancient Goddess Ceres. Some know me as Juno, some as Bellona, others as Hecate, others again as the Goddess of Rhamnus, but both races of Ethiopians, whose lands the morning sun first shines upon, and the Egyptians, who excel in ancient learning and worship me with their appropriate ceremonies, call me by my true name, Queen Isis. I have come in pity of your plight; I have come to favour and aid you. Weep no more, lament no longer; the day of deliverance, shone over by my watchful light, is at hand. (Lucius Apuelius, *The Golden Ass*, pg. 183)

There are a lot of things about this speech which interest me, but I think what interests me most of all are the words: 'You see me here', and 'I have come'. There is of course a lot going on in this ritual speech. We can see in this text a kind of monotheism, for the Goddess says that all the different goddesses in all the different places She mentions are Herself, the same goddess, under different names and faces. The Hindu god Krishna makes a similar claim as well in the Bhagavad Gita: many names, many faces, one deity. Yet the simple words 'I have come', constitute a logical formula for the assertion of presence. That is to say, the goddess *presents*Herself to someone with these words: She makes Herself known and *revealed* to someone.

Finally, consider the Coptic Christian text known to us today as *The Thunder, Perfect Mind*. It was discovered in 1945 among the Nag Hammadi scrolls. It's difficult to say what it is: on first reading, it appears to be an account of how God introduced Himself to the author of the text. (Perhaps I should say *Her*-self, since the speaker mainly uses female symbols here.) Part of it reads as follows:

...I am the first and the last.
I am the honored one and the scorned one.
I am the whore and the holy one.
I am the wife and the virgin.
I am [the mother] and the daughter.
I am the members of my mother.
I am the barren one, and many are her sons.
I am she whose wedding is great, and I have not taken a husband.
I am the midwife and she who does not bear.
I am the solace of my labour pains.
I am the bride and the bridegroom, and it is my husband who begot me.
I am the mother of my father, and the sister of my husband, and he is my offspring.
I am the slave of him who prepared me.
I am the ruler of my offspring, but he is the one who begot me before the time on a birthday.
And he is my offspring in (due) time, and my power is from

him.

I am the staff of his power in his youth, and he is the rod of my old age, and whatever he wills happens to me.

I am the silence that is incomprehensible, and the idea whose remembrance is frequent.

I am the voice whose sound is manifold, and the word whose appearance is multiple.

I am the utterance of my name.

(*The Nag Hammadi Library in English*, p. 297-8.)

Almost every sentence here is a logical absurdity. Perhaps this is what happens when one tries to imagine something which is defined in advance as unimaginable. It would seem the author is saying that if you could perceive God whole and in a single glance, you would find Her such an Immensity that no straight-forward categorical proposition will describe the experience. Thus one has to revert to paradoxes like these. Yet taken as a whole, there is a coherence and consistency between each statement which lends the text an interesting logic of its own. The speaker presents a sequence of paired opposites, which in the normal course of human life cannot be attributed to the same person at the same time: the condition of being mother to one's own father, for instance. We have to think differently about each proposition. Alternatively, each proposition might be cast in the form of a paradox in order to propel the mind into the realm of the abstract and the immaterial. With the material and social categories people normally rely upon suspended, what remains is the spirit. Yet whatever else is going on here, the speaker asserts that her presence can be discerned in and with each of these paradoxical characters. God *is* each of them. The last line in the passage quoted here interests me very much. Perhaps the writer had in mind the mysticism of the *Logos*, which appears in the first line of the Gospel of John: "In the beginning was the word, and the word was with God, and the word was God" [*En arche en ho Logos, kai ho Logos en pros ton Theon, kai Theos en ho Logos.]*. Yet here in *Perfect Mind* the word is not just any word: it is a *name*. Moreover, God identifies Herself not only with the name as such, but also with the act of speaking it. She is not just that to which words "I am here" refer; She is also that which you experience when the words are spoken. Thus She is not a 'thing', but an *event*.

The many names by which God is known, such as those by which Isis identified Herself, and the paradoxical characters in which God presents Herself in *The Thunder, Perfect Mind*, are perhaps all elaborations or extensions of this straightforward assertion of presence. They are all different ways of saying the same the basic message. Whatever the name, and whatever the mask and costume she wears, and whatever your spiritual path, She says to us all, 'I am here, close to you, here and now, where you can find me.'

§ 18. A Digression

Students of philosophy might recognise that my method here is similar to the phenomenology of Edmund Husserl, as described in his 1913 book *Logical Investigations*. His aim was to study consciousness, and to study it scientifically and philosophically, but to study it from the inside. To do this, he thought it necessary to first suspend "the natural attitude", meaning the ordinary, everyday, practical assumptions that we have about the things we see in the world. This act of suspension he called *epoché*, a term based on a Greek word which means 'standing back', 'withdrawal', or 'reduction'. To intellectually study his own consciousness, he had to stand back from something in his perceptual experiences. Having done that, he could examine what remained after that act of perceptual reduction had been done. To focus himself exclusively on the workings of his own mind, Husserl had to systematically suspend the belief in the existence of the world outside his mind. With that done, all that would remain would be the workings of his own thoughts and perceptions.

Husserl's *époche* is similar in some ways to the methodological doubt used by Rene Descartes in his *Meditations*. Like Husserl, Descartes wanted to know what the foundation of knowledge is. Thus he methodologically examined everything he thought he knew, and suspended everything that he had even the smallest reason to doubt. He did this in search of something he could not doubt. In this way he arrived at the famous *cogito ergo sum*, that is, the knowledge of his own existence, as a first-order phenomenological insight.

In the *epoché* that I'm using here, I'm suspending all the utilitarian associations that things appear to have. I'm standing back from all the ways in which we see things as useful, practical, belonging to someone, able to fulfill straightforward purposes.

In that way I can perceive what, if anything, remains, and what, if anything, is *essential* to that which I am perceiving. Imagine hearing the sound of a train whistle from a short distance away. When you hear this sound, and in your mind you suspend the knowledge that you are hearing a warning to other vehicles, what remains? When *all* of our perceptions of things in the world have been reduced like that, what remains? Clearly, only *presence* remains; only the knowledge that something is here and something is now, something is revealing its existence to us, and whatever it is, it is not nothing.

I'm also drawing on some of the investigative principles that belong to aesthetics, which is the branch of philosophy that investigates art, beauty, and the emotions. The word 'aesthetics' was crafted in 1735 by Alexander Baumgarten in his philosophical studies of art. He defined beauty as 'a sensible perfection'. It is sensible because it has to do with the activity of our senses: it is something to look at, to listen to, or touch. It is perfect because, as Baumgarten would have understood the meaning of the word 'perfect', it exists for its own sake. The work of art does not point to anything beyond itself, nor does it require the observer to assume anything other than what is presented. There does not need to be any reference to a cosmic or spiritual higher reality, of which the beautiful thing is merely a representation. The beautiful thing, on this understanding, is a whole world unto itself. Indeed Baumgarten uses that very simile: a work of art is like a world. Corresponding to the perfection of the work of art is the perfection of the aesthetic experience. The observer, in adopting an aesthetic attitude, suspends his or her utilitarian concerns of what the work is 'for'. He lets it be what it is. Having disengaged from utilitarian concerns, the person who beholds a work of art can become absorbed in it, even enraptured in it, and can enjoy the experience for its own sake, not for the sake of anything else that the person may care about. Contemporary philosopher Erwin Panofsky explained this principle as follows:

> When a man looks at a tree from the point of view of a carpenter, he will associate it with the various uses to which he might put the wood; and when he looks at it from the point of view of an ornithologist, he will associate it with the birds that might nest in it. When a man at a horse race watches the animal on which he has put his money, he will associate its performance with his desire that it may win. Only he who simply and wholly abandons himself to the object of his perception will experience it aesthetically. (Panofsky, *Meaning in the Visual Arts*, pg. 11.)

This understanding presupposes the phenomenology of Heidegger, who argued that all perceptions of the world are bound up with the observer's projects and interests. Yet Panofsky's idea here is that when we look at something *aesthetically*, we do not associate it or relate it to our interests and intentions. Indeed we do not associate it with anything other than itself. Rather, we just let it be itself. We let it speak to us on its own terms. We enjoy the sight of something that is complete in itself. If some part of it seems out of place or inconsistent compared to another part, then we go looking for how it fits into the totality. If we find that it does fit, we experience pleasure.

The aesthetic perception of things, in which we stand back (*epoché*) from utilitarian associations, is perhaps easiest to discern in vocal music performed in a language that you do not understand. In these cases, some of the work of *epoché* has been done for you already. The words might have a utilitarian reference, but the foreign-language listener won't get it. That level of meaning has been stripped away. To use Husserl's terms, it has been reduced. All that remains is the *sound*, and the knowledge that the sound was generated in the body of another living human being. In other words, all that remains is the assertion of the presence of the singer. It will be as if the singer is repeating the phrase "I am here!", once more and once again, many times over, in every harmonic variation possible. Some recent artists have explored this aesthetic experience by composing music using artificial languages of their own devising. Karl Jenkins' *Adeimus*, Vangelis' *Mythodia*, Lisa Gerrard's vocals as a member of Dead Can Dance, and the "Gregorian" Chant behind Eric Levi's *Era* and *The Mass*, are recent examples. The vocals sound like real languages, and some are based on real languages. But they are actually meaningless phonemes. They strip away the linguistic content of the sound, and enable the voice to be appreciated as a musical instrument in its own right. You could imagine that the song is a story, a confession, a joke, an apology, a wisdom teaching, a sacred oath, a dialogue with God. But all that truly remains is "I am here!"

I have been using cairns and songs as examples. But the Revelation could take almost any shape in which, alongside whatever other purposes are in play, someone communicates the fact of her own existence. Some ancient Aboriginal cultures communicate this fact by painting the outline of their hands on to cliff faces, cave walls, and great rocks. They filled their mouths with a plant-based pigment, put their hand on the rock, and spat the pigment out. The spatter would stain the rock, but leave the outline of the hand in the negative space. The modern urban version of the same is perhaps something like graffiti, on a railway boxcar, or the wall of a factory. I suppose that crop circles are someone's way of saying 'I am here', but nobody really knows who is saying it (although it's probably local pranksters). The Revelation can take just about any form in which someone leaves a kind of signature on the world, a sign of her presence in the world. It could be a painting, a story or a poem, a hand written letter, a stage play, a birthday gift, a phone message left on someone's answering service, a coin dropped into a fountain, a flower planted in a garden. The Revelation is implicit within each of these events. It is the primary assertion of presence which must of logical necessity accompany any other statement or exclamation one makes in the world. Try looking at the world without utilitarian associations for a while. You might be surprised at how quickly you start seeing and hearing Revelations of presence everywhere.

§ 19. "This is who I Am!"

Something should be said of the apparent fact that the Revelation always takes a definite practical form. It is always stated implicitly, as part of something else, and never in pure abstraction. In this way, the 'I am here!' reveals more than mere presence alone. The form of the Revelation always manifests as something definite and particular. It might be a cairn, or a song, but it is never a pure logical abstraction. In that way, the Revelation asserts not only presence, but also *identity*. It asserts that the maker has a specific history, a biography, a set of values, a set of purposes, a series of relationships, and everything else that goes into the way you can be distinguished from others. The 'I' of the 'I am here!' is not just any 'I'. Rather, it is the 'I' of he or she who speaks that 'I'. This can be seen in the very words used to describe the logical structure of the Revelation. They carry not just the assertion of my presence, but also particular information about my life. The simple fact that I am writing this book in English tells you something about where I came from, and the linguistic community in which I belong. If I were to say instead that the logical form of the Revelation is 'Je suis ici', or 'Ich bin hier', or 'Ben buradayim', then I would say something slightly different about who I am.

Presence appears in a practical and *identifiable* way – hence to speak of presence is also to speak of *identity*. Yet the two are not precisely the same. Presence is phenomenological, and existential; but identity is social, and sometimes political too. The 'I am here!' which appears in a Neolithic stone cairn is existentially and phenomenologically the same as that which appears in a modern steel and glass skyscraper. But the two buildings also embody different facts about the social world in which the builders lived. The most obvious of these will have to do with the technological power of the builders: the degree of engineering skill, the use of natural or synthetic materials, and so on. Just as in language, part of the message of the 'I am here!' is thus bound into the very instrument used to communicate that message. As Canadian philosopher Marshal McLuhan once said, "The medium is the message." It can be safely inferred that every Revelation is made in a way that also says something about who its maker is, where she comes from, what traditions or customs she has inherited, the technological power and social order of the society she lives in, and so on. It might not say much about all these facts, but it will certainly say something about a few of them. In this way, the person who asserts her presence does not assert just anyone's presence: she asserts *her own* presence. The Inukshuk is distinct to the Inuit people of northern Canada and the portal dolmen is distinctive to the Neolithic people of early Ireland. These things signify a definite people of a definite time and place. It signifies qualities which distinguish these people from other people. In other words, they signify *a way of being in the world*. They add a second term, a second *movement*, to the logical structure of the Revelation: 'I am here, and *this* is who I am!'

§ 20. The Invocation

As another example, think of invocations and prayers. When someone prays, she usually imagines that she is addressing the deity. Yet the most important element of prayer is the 'I am here!', the seed of the Revelation. Indeed this is the very element which makes it *prayer* instead of another kind of dramatic recitation. To see this, it may be useful to consider a prayer which perhaps most of you have never heard before, and certainly none of you have ever actually used.

In Geoffrey of Monmouth's *History of the Kings of Britain*, written in the early 12th century, we find the story of a band of refugees from the fall of Troy. As they travel the Mediterranean in search of a place to settle, they find a ruined city with a temple to the goddess Diana. The people suggest that their leader, Brutus, should consult the goddess for information about where they should go to find a new home. Brutus went to the temple, bringing with him a seer and "twelve of the older men". He made three sacrificial fires, poured four libation-offerings of wine and dog's blood into them, and then "he broke the silence" with this prayer:

> O powerful goddess, terror of the forest glades, yet hope of the wild woodlands, you who have the power to go in orbit through the airy heavens and the halls of hell, pronounce a judgement which concerns the earth. Tell me which lands you wish us to inhabit. Tell me of a safe dwelling-place where I am to worship you down the ages, and where, to the chanting of maidens, I shall dedicate temples to you. (*History of the Kings of Britain*, i.II, pg. 65)

Brutus recited this prayer nine times, and then laid out to sleep on the floor at the foot of the altar. In his dream that night the goddess Diana visited him, and She directed him to an island off the north-west coast of Europe. When they found the island, Brutus settled his people there, and named it after himself. Today, we call it the island of Britain.

The invocation which Geoffrey of Monmouth has kindly recorded for posterity was a special-purpose petition, of the sort scholars of religion call 'extemporaneous' prayer. He probably never prayed exactly like this ever again, since he certainly never had the same need ever again. But his petition follows a clear pattern which anyone from any religious tradition might recognise, even today. There is an 'I am here!', in the form of three sacrificial hearth-fires and a libation-offering to deity by whom he wishes to be heard. Next, he 'broke the silence' to address the deity with spoken words: first with praise for the deity's power, and an affirmation of the goodness of her personal qualities. Second, Brutus asked for some kind of help. Third and finally, he promised to do something in return if the help is granted: he promised to build temples in Diana's honour. In all of these movements in the prayer, Brutus does more than what the face-value interpretation would suggest. His sacrificial fires and the offerings he poured into them represent his Revelation, his assertion of presence. Yet in this assertion he also *declares a specific spiritual and cultural identity*. The very structure of the invocation tells us something about what he believes about the way to approach a deity, what he believes the deity can do for him and what he thinks She would want in return. The qualities for which he praises Diana are qualities he finds desirable and good in a deity. These, in turn, tell us something about the man himself, and something of his way of being in the world.

It is the same for almost any kind of prayer, including traditional texts which are recited more or less the same way each time. Consider, as an example, The Charge of the Goddess, by Doreen Valiente, one of the central ritual speeches in the religion of Wicca. It is phrased as an address from the deity to the believer, rather than from the believer to the deity, but you can still find all the elements of Revelation mentioned so far. It begins with a list of Goddesses, some from Greek and Roman mythology and some from the Celtic pantheon, and asserts that they are all faces of one comprehensive Goddess. The Charge includes guidelines for ritual, such as the suggestion that the best time for ritual is "once in a month... when the moon is full". It describes what the Goddess offers humanity: "knowledge of the spirit eternal", and what she requires in return: "ye shall dance, sing, feast, make music, and love, all in my praise". It enumerates eight specific character-virtues, in a series of paired opposites, which the Goddess asks the committed Wiccan to practice. Then it finishes by affirming the Goddess' presence in the soul of the Wiccan practitioner, and throughout all historical time.

Lest these examples give the impression that only ancient or minority religions follow this pattern, consider the way Christians address themselves to God using the Lord's Prayer. This ritual recitation establishes God's place in the cosmic order of things, and the believer's relationship to God ("Our Father, who art in Heaven"); and affirms that God's power is comprehensive ("Thy Will be done on earth as in heaven"). Then the prayer petitions God for help ("Give us this day our daily bread... deliver us from evil"). In return, the believer acknowledges God's authority over the world ("For thine is the kingdom, the power and the glory..."). The narrative structure is exactly the same as in Brutus' petition to the goddess Diana, and exactly the same as the Charge of the Goddess. Overall, the Lord's Prayer is essentially an elaborate and formal and yet magically powerful way for someone to assert that he is a Christian.

But this is only one instance of an even more universal theme. Every religious tradition with any maturity in it has statements of spiritual identity like this, even if the specific logical structure I have here described is only partly evident. The Al-Fatiha, the Shemah Yisrael, the Gayatri Mantra, the Peace of the Morrígan, the Universal Druid's Prayer, and any other expression of religious commitment like these, are all revelations of presence and identity. When *any* religious person recites a prayer to *any* deity, she does more than just ask for her daily bread. She also says, 'I am here, and this is who I am. And I am a person who believes the following things about the world and about my life. I live by the following values. I am committed to this path, and to the community of people who have the same commitments. I am empowered with the knowledge that as I say this prayer, thousands or even millions of people say it with me, and I am not alone.'

§ 21. The Way That Can Be Spoken

It is probably about time, now, that I defined this crucial term that I have been already using so loosely: 'a way of being in the world'. For practical purposes, your way of being in the world is who you are. It is your personal identity. Yet this simple definition, while I think it true, is not without problems. If asked to describe that identity, I could say, 'Well, this is what I do to work and rest and play; this is my history, these my purposes and these my hopes'. Most people also describe some of their public associations: you might say you are an uncle, an electrician, a dog owner, a resident of this town, a member of this church, or a citizen of this nation. Yet in response, someone might say, 'Well that's lovely, but that tells me *what* you are, and does not tell me *who* you are.' The matter of *who* you are is that which remains after the *epoché* has noted and suspended these practical public associations, which but for various turns of events could have been other than what they are. Even your name is among the accidents of your identity, for your parents could have named you differently. With all these things suspended, clearly only presence remains: 'I am she who is here, right now.' But at that level, you are perhaps indistinguishable from others: for that is the answer that *everyone* can offer in response to the question 'Who are you?'.

Such is the difficulty involved in defining the concept of a way of being in the world. But let us not give up too quickly. Your way of being is who you are; it is also a way of hearing and seeing things, a way of interpreting and understanding things, and a way of acting and doing things. Further, it is a way of doing these things which is distinctly and consistently *your* way, even as others may have a similar way. This is not simply, nor only, a way of making choices in each moment. Nor is it a rule or a principle by which one's choices are judged, like a court of appeal. Nor is it a matter of style or fashion. Nor is it an attitude that somehow affects one's perceptions and choices, as coloured glasses affect what one can see, or as the wood of a tree is affected by being fed through a machine. Rather, a way of being in the world is more like a group of habits or habitual postures from which one's actions, perceptions, and thoughts are launched. It more like a way of 'holding', or 'having', or 'possessing' one's own body and mind. It is that by reason of which one's actions and choices are intelligible, recognisable, consistent, and *one's own*. That is to say, they are expressive or representative of one's self. For selfhood is not a thing, nor is it a possession: it is an *activity* which takes place in the world.

Yet it resists description. Another part of the problem here is that an analytic description of your way of being in the world *is not your way of being in the world*. Such a description can only offer clinical facts about identity: it cannot deliver the living presence of the person. Perhaps Lao Tzu began his great philosophical teaching, the *Tao Te Ching*, with the same problem in mind: "The Tao that can be spoken is not the Tao." A description is a collection of words, while a way of being in the world is a collection of habits, thoughts, feelings, choices, experiences, values, and deeds. Thus a way of being in the world is evasive and mysterious. We know of its presence, and we can *see* it in action, yet as soon as we try to talk about it, we find it dwells in silence and darkness. I know perfectly well what my way of being in the world is, until someone asks me to explain it. This prompts the question: How can it be both a presence and a mystery at the same time?

Here is one possible answer, as it appeared in Dante Gabriel Rossetti's *Sonnets from the House of Life*:

And though thy soul sail leagues and leagues beyond—
Still, leagues beyond those leagues, there is more sea.

As it is for exploring the coastlines of the earth during the age of sail, so it is for exploring what it is to be human. It is not that a way of being in the world cannot be described at all. It is that any description of someone or something's way of being in the world can never account for everything. However much it is described, there will always be more that is not yet described. However much is said, there is always more to say. Thus it is not the evasiveness of things which make them mystical. It is not the mystery of things which makes them spiritual. Rather, things are mystical if they offer a continuing never-ending Revelation. Things are spiritual if they offer an ongoing, ever-unfolding presence. To the extent that every person's way of being in the world admits of no end to its potential description, every way of being in the world has a dimension that is mystical, and spiritual.

§ 22. "And What I Am Is Beautiful!"

The Revelation has a third movement.

Some of the decisions that must go into building an inukshuk and a portal dolman are obviously structural in nature. The base has to be strong enough to support the top. Yet there are some elements here which have nothing to do with engineering. How big should it be? Should it resemble a person, as an inukshuk does? Should it resemble a gateway, like a portal dolman? Should it resemble a geometric shape, like a stone circle? Architects are very interested in the artistic qualities of their buildings as well as in their functional suitability. Strictly speaking, it is not possible to design a building entirely in a 'form follows function' kind of way. There are always non-instrumental and non-utilitarian features. As the architecture critic Hans Hollein put it, "Form does not follow function. Form does not arise out of its own accord. It is the great decision of man to make a building as a cube, a pyramid, or a sphere." (Hollein, *Changing Ideas in Modern Architecture*, pg. 182.) A similar point may be applied to the work of potters, carpenters, stonemasons, and any number of skilled artisans who create with their hands. They too are very interested in elements of design and ornamentation which are not strictly practical in nature. That part of the things we make which of necessity does *not* follow from its utilitarian function, nor from the requirements of structural engineering, must presumably follow from something else. What might it be?

Similarly, in music there are technical elements that may be compared to the engineering requirements of architecture. In music, the rhythm has to be consistent and recognisable. The melody has to employ principles of harmonic relation: major fourths, major fifths, relative minors, augmented chords, diminished chords, and so on. Harmonic relations are grounded in the physics of sound waves, and the way that sound waves of different frequencies propagate or interfere with each other. Rhythm is grounded in the world through biology: the heartbeat, the breath, the walking pace, the relative sizes of our bones (which resonate with sounds of different frequencies), other motions of the limbs, perhaps also the frequency of electro-chemical signals in the brain and the nervous system. Yet the excellence of music is not contingent upon following the require-ments of these physical and organic foundations. It is the composer's great decision that a piece of music should be in the key of C, or the key of F, or that its time signature should be a jig, a reel, a hornpipe. Nothing in the physics of sound or the functions of biology dictates that the composer should write a symphony instead of a sea shanty, or that a musician should play the marimba instead of the heavy metal guitar. Moreover, composers can deliberately subvert the technical elements by using dissonant chords, or nonstandard rhythms, or even by changing rhythms and home chords part way through the piece. And of course the finest performances have a certain hard to define emotional and evocative power, which perhaps is only tangentially related to technical perfection. Just as in architecture, something else is at work here too. So what is it?

On one level, the 'something else' at work here might be just the arbitrary free choice of the architect or the composer. But I think that cannot be all. Someone who builds a cairn or writes a song has to make choices. Someone who recites a prayer, even if the words are given by tradition, had to decide which prayer to recite. When you hear someone sing, or find a cairn on your path, you can perceive its creator's will, embodied in stone, manifest in sound. A Revelation 'reveals' its creator's will to create in some particular way. In this part of the Revelation, where decision is involved, principles of ethics appear; principles of aesthetics also. In examples like prayers the moral dimension may be obvious since the very words themselves may be affirmations of moral values. Yet this dimension exists in every assertion of presence that anyone might make, in any medium. For behind the decision to build a cairn in the shape of a man, or in the shape of a gateway, is the decision that *a cairn shall be built*. And behind that decision is the deeper, ethical-aesthetic judgment that *it is good to build cairns in this way*. Behind the decision to sing an opera by Mozart, or a folk song by Stan Rogers, or a wordless improvisation in a jazz performance, is the decision that *a song shall be performed*. And behind that decision lies the ethical-aesthetic judgment that *it is good to sing in this way*. Without that moral judgement, you would make a different kind of assertion of presence and identity; or, alternatively, you wouldn't do anything.

Thus we have a third movement in the phenomenological structure of Revelation. It asserts presence, and it asserts identity, as already seen: but what is more, it asserts its creator's *will to the desirability of life*. It is a moral-aesthetic proposition, and it takes the following logical form:

> ...I was a Flower of the mountain yes when I put the rose in my hair like the Andalusian girls used or shall I wear a red yes and how he kissed me under the Moorish wall and I thought well as well him as another and then I asked him with my eyes to ask again yes and then he asked me would I yes to say yes my mountain flower and first I put my arms around him yes and drew him down to me so he could feel my breasts all perfume yes and his heart was going like mad and yes I said yes I will Yes. (James Joyce, *Ulysses*, ch. 18)

Here, in this moment of the Revelation, the will *delights* in itself as it asserts itself: it *revels* in the revel-ation of its existence. Here we can have all manner of personal celebrations and festivities, with all the noise and shenanigans that may come. It might be a birthday, a sporting victory, a marriage, a school graduation, the completion of a special project. But whatever the occasion for celebration might be, it is a part of life and an experience of life: thus every celebration also implies a celebration of life and of being alive. Wherever you find the assertion of 'I am here!' *enjoyed* by she who asserts it, you find this third movement of the Revelation: the assertion of the ethical desirability of life.

To the two movements of the logical formula of the Revelation, "I am here, and this is who I am!", we now add the third term: "and what I am is beautiful!"

§ 23. Another Digression

For centuries philosophers gave themselves the task of finding a reason why a virtuous life ('virtuous' in the original intention of the word: a life that is excellent, and fitting for a human being) is more satisfying, more desirable, and generally *better* than the life of a fool, a sloth, a vulgarot, or a criminal. It might be argued that a good man has fewer enemies, or that a good man is more likely to be shown mercy and generosity, or that the good man is generally happier, or that the bad man usually dies alone. It is likely that each of these assertions are merely expressions of the prejudices of each author's time and place. But I have no objection to any of them. Indeed I believe they are all true. Yet I am chasing a different kind of animal. I'm hunting for a reason to affirm *the ethical desirability of life*. I seek a reason why it is desirable for life to go on, and why it is better to be alive than to have never been born in the first place. I seek a reason why someone who fully and honestly grasps the inherent loneliness of existence should not cave in to despair, nor retreat into illusion, nor succumb to madness or suicide.

It seems to me that utilitarian arguments are not good enough for the purpose. In the Utilitarian way of thinking, the right decision is the one in which the benefits that result from it outweigh the harms. For most sorts of practical moral decisions, this is an excellent principle to use. But I think it can give only marginally useful answers to the most serious and deepest of our philosophical problems. When asked whether life is ethically desirable, a utilitarian might try to show that the benefits of staying alive outweigh the problems. But someone else, with very different life experiences, might weigh the utility of events differently. Certainly a suicidal person (as a Utilitarian would understand him) is one who has apparently decided that the problems of his life do outweigh the benefits. He therefore chooses death in order to prevent the continuation of suffering. Pressed further to state whether life is ethically desirable, a utilitarian might argue that a universe like ours, with its changing mix of happiness and suffering, might nonetheless be preferable to a universe with no life in it at all. But this can be questioned too. Our world can only be preferable so long as the total happiness outweighs the total suffering. There cannot be a question of the *inherent* desirability of life. The Utilitarian might tweak his calculus, and claim that being alive is a benefit that can always outweigh the burdens and problems of life. But this introduces a non-Utilitarian principle into the argument, namely, a mysterious claim about the inherent goodness of being alive. This principle should be *explained* rather than haphazardly thrown in for the sake of solving a logic puzzle. Finally, the Utilitarian might argue that our world, such as it is, might be comparatively better than nothing. But this argument runs into that old contradiction of language again. 'Nothing', as such, is neither better nor worse than any alternative state of affairs. Nor is it better or worse than existence as such. Nothing is *nothing*. There are no terms of comparison. It is therefore logically impossible to claim that something is better or worse than nothing. But that is precisely what must be claimed in order to assert the ethical desirability of life.

In the absence of Utilitarian thinking, what remains? Perhaps life is ethically desirable because God has willed it so. But this seems to me all too easy. It merely inserts the idea of God into the place of the very question that needs to be explained, and thus lets one escape the real work of explaining it.

What matters is not whether God finds life ethically desirable. *What matters is whether we do.* It seems to me that the strongest reason why life is desirable is because, somewhere in the world, someone has declared it so by an act of will. That someone cannot be God: it has to be someone living an embodied life. For only a person living an embodied life is in a position to know what embodied life is, and in a position to decide, one moment to the next, whether life is worth continuing. For such a person, the question of the ethical desirability of life is a relevant question. Molly Bloom says Yes, not only to her Andalusian lover, but to *all of life itself*. Perhaps more than any observation of things, it is a willful Yes, like hers, which makes life desirable and good.

§ 24. The Will

Shades of Perscriptivism are evident here. This is a type of relativism which states that a moral principle is only what someone says it is. There need not be any appeal to nature, or divine command, or to experiences like harm or benefit, nor to pure reason. The only foundation for any moral principle is the *will* of the person who asserts it. Similarly, when someone makes choices and lives life in a certain way, he effectively declares that his way of choosing and living is a morally correct way to choose and to live. Thus, a statement like 'stealing is wrong' really means 'I hereby prescribe that stealing is wrong', and that is all there is to say about it. This leads to a certain arbitrariness. (Oddly enough, that is precisely what God does when he prescribes the Ten Commandments. But I digress.)

If the discourse on Revelation was only an elaborate and complicated form of perscriptivism, then it would be open to some obvious and serious objections. For instance, many people do things they know very well are morally questionable, if not clearly harmful to themselves and others. The person who is addicted to alcohol, or who gives nothing to charities even though he is wealthy, or who drives his car recklessly, or who sires a dozen children by as many different women, is perhaps prescribing his own rules for himself. His choices might be unhealthy, selfish, risky, thoughtless, callous, or cold-hearted, but at least they are his own.

I think, however, that the ethical prescription of the Revelation has to be something life affirming, and I think there is a certain logical necessity in this. The ethical moment in the Revelation is the moment when a person honours herself, affirms the goodness of the life she is living, and the goodness of the world she is living in. I think this is implicitly accomplished in the very act of cairn-building, or musical performance, or any of the things that might go into a non-suicidal way of being in the world. By doing such things, the will implicitly affirms that those things are *worth doing*. The alternative is not a different kind of Revelation: the alternative is *no* Revelation – and thus a retreat into loneliness again.

I am using the word 'life' as a fundamental category of ethical value here. Yet as such the word might still be ambiguous: for instance, it means one thing to a pro-life activist, and another to a pro-choice activist. What does it mean in terms of the Revelation; indeed, what *should* it mean? Allow me to clarify that when I speak of life as a moral category, I'm not speaking of one or other side of the political debate on abortion, or euthanasia, or doctor-assisted suicide. I'm speaking of the worth and the value one assigns to one's own embodied existence. I also speak of embodied organic existence on Earth in general, whether it is human, or whether it is animal, or plant, or insect, or microbe, or any other form that organic life takes. And I speak of all the ecological relations among life-forms in the planetary biosphere. If knowledge and imagination reaches far enough, we can include the cosmic environment of interstellar space. In particular, I speak of the moment of the Revelation when, by an act of will, you resolve that life on Earth is worthwhile and valuable, *even as it is lonely*. The will must affirm the ethical desirability of life even as life is sometimes full of misery, conflict, ugliness, and insipid banality. This can often be an act of heroism and of courage. You have to honestly evaluate your life, including all the things in it which make it frustrating and hard. It is like shaking one's fist at a thundercloud, or gazing into an abyss. It acknowledges the danger therein: the wind and the lightning, the long fall into darkness. It acknowledges the hypnotic effect of these immensities, which can create an absurd desire to throw oneself into them. This latter sensation is often experienced by visitors to mountains, canyons, and deep gorges. The Cliffs of Moher, in Ireland, for example, are several kilometers long, and reach 200 meters above the Atlantic Ocean. For much of their length, there are no physical barriers to prevent the casual visitor from falling to her death. Many visitors feel an irrational yet compelling desire to deliberately throw themselves over the edge. What a simple, easy, even *elegant* way to solve all of one's problems! How easy to imagine one would float away like an autumn leaf, and gently disappear into the mist. Of course the visitor also knows the reality is that he would directly plummet to a sharp reception. Nonetheless, some people in troubled times in their lives contemplate whether a half-second of physical pain might be better than enduring the rest of their lives. What holds them back from doing this is the desire to continue living: what supports this desire for life is the implicit resolution that life is worth living, and the world worth living in.

§ 25. The First of All Moral Judgments

Aristotle wrote that the love of oneself is a moral priority. But he also carefully distinguishes good from bad forms of self-love. The self-love of a bad person, he says, manifests itself as irrational greed for material wealth and public fame. Here is the argument in his own words:

> Those then who make it a term of reproach call men lovers of self when they assign to themselves the larger share of money, honours, or bodily pleasures; since these are the things which most men desire and set their hearts on as being the greatest goods, and which accordingly they compete with each other to obtain. Now those who take more than their share of these things are men who indulge their appetites, and generally their passions and the irrational part of their souls. But most men are of this kind. Accordingly the use of the term 'lover of self' as a reproach has arisen from the fact that self-love of the ordinary sort is bad. (*Nicomachean Ethics* 9.viii.4)

Yet Aristotle does not say that the opposite of the selfish man is the self-sacrificing man. Rather, he says that there is a positive, ethically praiseworthy kind of self-love:

> For if a man was always bent on outdoing everybody else in acting justly or temperately or in displaying any of the virtues, and in general were always trying to secure for himself moral nobility, no one would charge him with love of self or find any fault with him. Yet as a matter of fact such a man might be held to be a lover of self in an exceptional degree. At all events he takes for himself the things that are noblest and most truly good. Also it is the most dominant part of himself that he indulges and obeys in everything. (*ibid*, 9.viii.4)

Aristotle's argument may seem strange to us today, since it rests on the idea that the human soul has different parts, from which are launched different kinds of desires. Aristotle's teacher, Plato, wrote that each person has three souls, not just one, and Aristotle himself followed this theory closely, although with minor variations. The first part of the soul is called the *appetitive* part: it is responsible for material desires, such as the desire to eat, or for material wealth and comfort. The second is called the *spirited* part of the soul. It inspires people to do great and heroic things, and it desires immaterial rewards like honour and fame. The third part of the soul is the *rational*. It is the seat of our intellectual understanding of things; it desires knowledge and wisdom. Plato also presented empirical evidence for this argument. Early in *The Republic*, Plato describes a man who felt himself compelled to look upon a pile of human corpses, yet at the same time felt disgusted with himself for wanting to do so. Plato's explanation for that odd behaviour was that the man's appetitive soul was competing with his rational soul. Happiness, according to Plato, is the condition of a person whose various souls are acting in proper relationship to each other. He also claims that the rational part of the soul has to dominate the others. When the appetitive soul dominates, people become miserly, greedy, and obsessed with the pursuit of material wealth. It is better when the spirited part is in charge, because the spirited soul can inspire people to benefit each other. But the spirited part of the soul can be dangerous too, for instance when it desires glory on a battlefield, or is prepared to act recklessly and destructively for the sake of public prominence. (Think of that fellow whose name I can't remember, who shot John Lennon precisely to tie his name to Lennon's life story and thus make himself famous.) It is best of all, Plato says, when the rational part of the soul is in charge. The rational part of the soul, Aristotle says, is the dominant part, because "it is our reasoned acts that are felt to be in the fullest sense *our own* acts, *voluntary* acts." A good man, who loves himself in the right kind of way, "values this [rational] part of himself most. Hence the good man will be a lover of self in the fullest degree." (*NE* 9.viii.6). Aristotle finally concludes this discussion by saying:

> The good man ought to be a lover of self, since he will then benefit both himself by acting nobly and aid his fellows; but the bad man ought not to be a lover of self, since he will follow his base passions, and so injure both himself and his neighbours. (*NE*, 9.viii.6)

In this early Greek way of thinking, the opposite of the self-loving man is not a self-denying man, but a different kind of self-loving man. The right kind of self-love is good for oneself and others too, and is thus morally praiseworthy. This last quoted statement may appear very utilitarian, since it brings the notion of 'harm' into play, and the notion that good people are useful to themselves and others. But actually Aristotle is invoking an idea, already ancient in his own time, that moral excellence is self-rewarding and moral viciousness self-punishing. He is not comparing possible outcomes of various choices. Rather, he is saying something about the logic of certain ways of being in the world.

I think this desire for life is the root of the ethical moment of the Revelation. The person who says 'I am here, and this is who I am', in whatever way she says it, must presuppose that her presence, identity, and way of being *deserves* to be revealed. She must presuppose the goodness of that which is revealed, and the rightness of the way it is revealed. To live at all, you have to presuppose, as a first-order proposition, that your own life is valuable, and worth continuing. This is not a matter of reciting a positive self-help affirmation: this is a matter of *doing something with your life*. Whatever it is you are doing right now *other than* committing suicide, or other than ruining your life some other way, is your de-facto assertion of the worth and the value of your life. Thus the Revelation adds to presence and identity a moral judgment: 'it is good to be alive, good to be here on earth, good to be who I am, right here, and right now.'

§ 26. The Examined Life

It can be useful, from time to time, to look into yourself, assess your life, and evaluate whether your life's history so far is that of a person who finds life desirable. It can be useful to do this on a fairly regular basis. In my own life, I find the best time to do so is around my birthday. But I also do so whenever I'm facing a decision that would significantly change the direction of my life. Socrates said, "The unexamined life is not worth living". I think he meant to say that the person who doesn't examine his life is easily swayed by fashion, and the opinions of the people around him, and is easily carried off by his instincts and emotions. Therefore he isn't in control of his own life, and thus he has no way of knowing whether or not his life is truly worthwhile.

The criteria for examining one's life are very simple: they take the form of diagnostic questions. When I reveal myself to others, what do I actually reveal? Does the history of my life actually reflect the proposition that life is desirable, beautiful, and good? Which of my habits, and relationships, and recent decisions do reflect this proposition, and which do not? And to what extent, and to what degree? Have I yet become the person I wish to be? Through questions like these, the fears, doubts, anxieties, and disturbances which sometimes emerge from the night watch can become catalysts for self-examination, and perhaps also change. If you look at yourself and don't like what you see, what will you do about it?

In this way, the logical form of the Revelation, "I am here, this is who I am, and what I am is beautiful!", may be distinguished from the pop-psychology affirmation, and from other forms of neuro-linguistic programming. The affirmation is expressed in the mode of a factual claim: "I'm good enough, I'm smart enough, and (dog-gone-it), people like me." It attempts to retroactively sanctify the choices you have already made, whatever they may be. But if the affirmation does not fit the actual facts of your life, you will end up making yourself feel worse. The Revelation, by contrast, is not merely spoken in words. It is spoken in deeds and choices and habits, and in one's whole way of being in the world. The Revelation of presence and identity is the reality of what we are, whatever that might be, and whether we like it or not. And the Revelation of ethically desirable life looks forward in time, not backwards; it is perhaps better to compare it to an oath. One who affirms the ethical desirability of life resolves to examine her life, direct her life in a certain way, and perhaps also *to change her life*, from that moment forward.

Before you continue reading this book, take a moment to ask yourself these questions. Don't wait until after your favourite TV show is finished. Do it right now.

§ 27. The Terrorist

Let us now consider another kind of problem. Nothing I have said so far rigorously excludes the possibility that an act of exploitation or of terror could be a Revelation. A particularly depraved individual might think he needs to oppress and victimize others in order to know that he is something-and-not-nothing. There is no shortage of examples of this kind of behaviour. In December of 1989 Marc Lepine entered L'Ecole Polytechnique in Montreal, and murdered fourteen women. His violence was frightening not only for its viciousness, but also for the sexual politics that motivated it. Lepine separated the men from the women, let the men go free, and killed only the women. He roamed the corridors of the building shouting "I want women!". In the final classroom, the students who he held as hostages were women enrolled in the engineering program, a traditionally male dominated profession. He told them that he hated them because they were feminists. When one said that they were not feminists but just students taking engineering, he shot three of them, and then shot himself. ("Gunmen massacres 14 women" *CBC News*, first broadcast 6th December, 1989.) On 27th July 2008, Jim Adkisson shot nine people in the Tennessee Valley Unitarian Universalist Church, killing two of them. Since he expected to be killed by the police, he wrote a suicide letter in which he expressed his hatred for the philosophy of liberalism, and for anyone who votes for the U.S. Democratic party. He also urged others to do as he had done, saying: "If life ain't worth living anymore, don't just kill yourself. Do something for your country before you go. Go kill liberals." (Jamie Satterfield, "Church shooter pleads guilty; letter released" *Knoxville News Sentinel*, 10th February 2009.) Adkisson and Lepine were politically motivated terrorists. But their actions were not at a loss for Revelation. They certainly made their presence known.

Let us simply observe that these attacks also assert the presence and the identity of the perpetrators, and thus count as Revelations, as I have defined the event so far. The logic is the same for the building of stone cairns and the singing of folk songs. Indeed some of the people who stage public shooting attacks do so precisely in order to be seen and known by others, and sometimes also to be seen and known by the mass media. That need to be seen is what apparently motivated the gunmen of the Columbine High School shooting near Littleton Colorado (1999), the Virginia Polytechnic Institute in Blacksburg Virginia (2007), and the Northern Illinois University shooting (2008). The two shooters at Columbine appear also to have been motivated by various forms of misanthropy: Harris was moved by narcicism and superiority, and Klebold by suicidal depression. (Greg Toppo, "10 years later, the real story behind Columbine" *USA Today*, 16th April 2009). But Let us not dwell overlong on psychological explanations for their actions. The point is that if the discourse on Revelation ended here, evil would receive a spiritual dimension.

I think it is evident that so long as the will is involved, an element of perscriptivism will always be present. It will always be possible, therefore, that someone could make violence his mode of asserting presence and identity. However, as seen in the previous meditation, the self-love presupposed in the Revelation must be logically consistent with itself, as a minimal requirement to avoid arbitrariness. A sociopath might speak nobly about individual rights, and the injustice of social and legal forces that weaken those rights, as he barricades himself into his house with a rifle and some hostages. His rhetoric only disguises a kind of narcissistic obsession with personal revenge and vigilante justice. Yet there is something self-defeating in this obsession. As he inflicts fear and pain on others in the service of his 'rights', he usually worsens his own problems. Indeed he usually and quickly sees that there is no way out of the environment of fear he creates around himself. It is perhaps ironically consistent, therefore, that some such criminals eventually turn their weapons on themselves, or else target the police in the last few moments, in the hope of going down in a blaze of glory.

More than two thousand years ago, the Chinese philosopher Lao Tzu observed, "Violent and fierce people do not die a natural death." (*Tao Te Ching*, ch. 42) The ancient wisdom that evil is self-defeating still rings true today. Therefore, the will to life must, as a basic moral norm, reject misanthropy, and any other values which lead to a self-refuting end. Moreover, the Revelation must also acknowledge the personhood of those who might see and hear it. There is a fundamental contradiction between communication and killing. It simply makes no sense to say you are communicating something to someone, when the recipient of your message must die to hear it. For once that kind of message is delivered, there is suddenly no one there to receive it. As Lévinas says, "to kill is not to dominate but to annihilate". (Lévinas, *Totality and Infinity*, pg. 198.) It follows that a 'communication' which entails the death of the recipient is no communication at all. Someone who says 'I am here!' using gunfire quickly finds that the dead cannot hear him, and so he remains just as isolated in his own world as before.

The same point arises for any 'communication' which robs the recipient of his humanity, dignity, and freedom, even if it does not kill. An industrialist who thinks of the workers as mere factors of production, or a sub-prime mortgage salesman who thinks his customers are gullible idiots, or a parent who thinks of his children as his property-possessions, or anyone who asserts his values by turning people into non-persons, commits a similar logical contradiction. He extends the hand of his power over others, and manipulates their lives, but once he grasps their freedom in his hand it vanishes. For exploitation is not communication: it is domination. Furthermore, someone who treats others as non-persons soon finds himself in a world with fewer and fewer persons in it. Thus he consigns himself to loneliness, almost as surely as if he went to live in a cave by himself. Perscriptivism, as a form of relativism, thus has it its limits. At the very least, it must not prescribe misanthropy. It must acknowledge in others the desire for life which it claims to possess in itself.

§ 28. The Personal Task

I described this requirement for non-contradiction in part to avoid the arbitrariness of relativism. I also wanted to show that the discourse on the Revelation which I have been building here can understand and fight evil. Yet to show the contradictions in the alternatives is not, by itself, quite enough to establish an argument for the ethical desirability of life. The will cannot just avoid the negative: it must also affirm something positive. It's never enough to work against something; one must also work *for* something. Is there anything in the notion of the will to life which is not just a matter of avoiding contradiction? Is there anything genuinely and perhaps even *independently* valuable about life, which deserves to be affirmed so?

To answer this, let's see if the *epoché* can be applied to the act of will itself. Immanuel Kant did just such a thing in his *Groundwork to the Metaphysics of Morals*, first published in 1785. In a discussion of different kinds of imperatives, Kant makes an interesting claim of value theory: "Who wills the end, wills...also the means which are indispensably necessary and in his power". (*Groundwork* pg. 84-5) In order for me to will some end, I must also be able to will the causes of that end. For example, if it is my will to make bread, it must also be my will to fetch water, flour, eggs, and to knead the dough, and to maintain my baking oven, and so on. If I trace back the things 'necessary and in my power' far enough, I ultimately find I must be able to will *my own will* as foremost among the various causes. Humanity as the "supreme limiting condition of all subjective ends" is placed in the position of that which is to be willed, the principle that limits all other principles. In other words, the will to life must affirm *itself* among all things to be affirmed.

This is the only sequence of reasoning in the text of the *Groundwork* for attributing intrinsic value exclusively to humanity, other than the discussion of freedom and the will. Elsewhere, humanity as an end in itself, and the will as the only thing that can be considered good without qualification, is simply assumed without supporting argument. Indeed he says early in the work that the concept of the will as an intrinsic good needs only to be clarified, not argued, as if it is a concept that is self-evidently true and which any rational being may grasp. Here are his words:

This concept [of the will as good in itself, apart from any further end], which is already present in a sound natural understanding and requires not so much to be taught as merely to be clarified, always holds the highest place in estimating the total worth of our actions and constitutes the condition of all the rest. (*Groundwork*, pg. 64-5.)

This suggests to me that Kant thought he had hit upon a first-order phenomenological insight.

Although Kant's philosophy is very different from Aristotle's, Kant wrote of the moral priority to love oneself in the right kind of way. Specifically, Kant also wrote of the moral duty to preserve one's own dignity. In his *Lectures on Ethics*, (a collection of lecture notes assembled posthumously by his students), he said "the prior condition of our duty to others is our duty to ourselves; we can fulfill the former only insofar as we first fulfill the latter." (*Lectures* pg. 118) As he explains it, each person has a duty to himself to do nothing which would undermine his dignity, and that this is a prerequisite to all other duties. "We must also be worthy of our manhood; whatsoever makes us unworthy of it makes us unfit for anything, and we cease to be men." (*Lectures* pg. 110) Again, we find an ethical necessity to affirm the goodness and desirability of life, starting with one's own life, implicit within whatever other purposes or values we might wish to affirm.

§ 29. The Social Task

This principle of self and life affirmation can extend further, like the expanding ripples on the surface of a pond. It continues on from the individual to the social and political dimensions of life. British scholar Kenneth Clark wrote that that a society becomes a civilisation when it affirms itself in a similar kind of way. Here are his words:

> ...civilisation requires a modicum of material prosperity – enough to provide a little leisure. But, far more, it requires confidence – confidence in the society in which one lives, belief in its philosophy, belief in its laws, and confidence in one's own mental powers. The way in which the stones of the Pont du Gard are laid is not only a triumph of technical skill, but shows a vigorous belief in law and discipline. Vigour, energy, vitality: all the great civilisations – or civilising epochs – have had a weight of energy behind them. (Clark, *Civilisation*, pg. 4)

Clarke is a historian, and so his statement here is meant as an observation, not a moral imperative. He presents quite a bit of evidence for this conclusion, more than I have space to repeat here. Yet it seems to me that the confidence in life which Clark speaks of is very close to the moral claims by Kant and Aristotle discussed earlier. Clark's claim is that great civilisations are vigorous, energetic, self-assured. One may infer that societies which don't become fully fledged civilisations are societies which lack this confidence. Indeed Clark makes a similar claim when he observes that civilisations don't really fall, but rather they become exhausted.

Albert Schweitzer, writing half a century earlier, also noted that great civilisations have confidence in themselves. But where

Clark noted this as a simple observation, Schweitzer cast it in the form of a moral imperative. And instead of grounding his argument in a claim about logic, as Kant did, Schweitzer expressed it in the form of a warning. Here are his words:

> The future of civilisation depends on our overcoming the meaninglessness and hopelessness which characterize the thoughts and convictions of men today, and reaching a state of fresh hope and fresh determination. We shall be capable of this, however, only when the majority of individuals discover for themselves both an ethic and a profound and steadfast attitude of world- and life-affirmation, in a theory of the universe at once convincing and based on reflection. Without such a general spiritual experience there is no possibility of holding our world back from the ruin and disintegration towards which it is being hastened. It is our duty then to rouse ourselves to fresh reflection about the world and life. (Schweitzer, *The Decay and Restoration of Civilisation*, pg. 8)

According to Schweitzer, if a society does not affirm the desirability of life as a basic ethical truth, then it will fall into a kind of torpor, and render itself vulnerable to disaster. One could look at this argument in a utilitarian way. Perhaps Schweitzer is saying that of the two possibilities, the attitude of life-affirmation causes more benefit and less harm to people than the alternative, and is therefore morally preferable. But I think Schweitzer's argument is not just a Utilitarian comparison of outcomes. I think he is also affirming that civilisation has to have confidence in itself as an inherently desirable condition.

§ 30. The Green Man

Can the circle be expanded even further? Is there anything in *organic life on Earth* which, on its own terms, renders life beautiful and good, and deserves to be affirmed so?

As I write these words, the season of springtime is arriving in my hometown. The snow is gone, the rains are washing away the last of the sand, road salt, and grit of winter. The wind is more gentle. Birds and insects are returning, trees are budding on the tips of their branches where new leaves will soon sprout. All over the world, it seems, small green shoots are emerging from the earth, and flowers are opening, and the sun is shining. When I lived in the west of Ireland, whenever I had a free afternoon I would walk along the coast path on the north shore of Galway Bay. Sometimes if it had been raining that afternoon, but was only partly cloudy by evening, the atmosphere would still be moist with soft mist, barely noticeable. Beams of sunshine pierced the air, moving slowly with the moving clouds and the setting sun. The rain-wetted stone of the Burren, which I could see across the bay, would gently glow with the colours of the sunset, and this light would reflect up to the clouds above, causing them to glow from below with the same warm light. As nightfall approached, the surface of the sea faded into the colour of the sky, making the coast across the bay seem to float, as if in a netherworld space, not part of this mortal world. The Arran Islands, too, floated in this magical light, and seemed as if they were not islands but ships in space, following the sun to the Otherworld.

Experiences like these can be treated as evidence that *the life of the earth makes its own Revelation*. The beauty of the earth is there to be seen. It is something that you must deliberately look for, and perhaps also something you must learn to see. Yet it is also something which can catch you unawares. Your attention can be drawn to it, your everyday routine interrupted by it. Not without evidence did Schopenhauer say that the will is universal, and that a human will is but an instance of a cosmic will which dwells in every moving, changing, and living thing in the world. In the wonders of the natural world, it can seem as if there are spiritual beings in the earth and the sun, asserting their presence to us, telling us that life is beautiful and good. It is the same for every birdsong, every flower, every warm summer breeze, every wave that falls on the shore. Any and every movement of energy which sustains and empowers the life of organisms and even whole ecosystems can be a Revelation that life is beautiful and good.

I'm obviously not the first philosopher to assert the idea that the natural world is a source of spiritual inspiration. Aboriginal people have held the life of the Earth in high spiritual esteem for centuries. In modern European philosophy it probably begins with Jean Jacques Rousseau. In American thought it is almost as old, and more or less begins with writers like Henry David Thoreau, and John Muir. Yet the force of this proposition isn't obvious to its anthropocentric opponents. They might argue that the proposition should be put to the test of perception: or in other words, the Revelation should be something that one can *see or hear*.

Consider, therefore, a wild apple tree in the full flower of springtime, in an open meadow. It is wonderfully beautiful, and few people would doubt this. The tree doesn't think of who or what will see its presence. It simply *is*. It doesn't display its flowers *to* anyone, nor *for* anyone. It would do this exactly the same way even if no one was there to see it happen. We could understand its blooming in a scientific way: many generations of natural selection have hit upon and propagated that particular method for attracting pollinating insects, and thus reproducing itself. Yet just as we can phenomenologically stand back from the utilitarian concerns of human architecture, as I explained before, so we can stand back from the evolutionary and reproductive function of the flowers. In the *epoché* mode of perception, even the biological imperatives, as explanations for the things we see, are set aside. Then we can simply *see* the flowers on the apple true just as they are in the present moment. If it does not reveal itself *to* anything nor *for* anything, then what remains?

One possible answer is that it grows and flowers for no reason. It just does what it does, and there is no 'why'. The tree in itself might be just a tree, and we see it as beautiful because we *will* ourselves to see it that way. And we do that because we cannot bear the thought that there is no reason for it to be there. If the tree exists for no reason, that might mean that other things exist for no reason too, perhaps including our own selves. Even in moments of beauty, there is a touch of loneliness.

But there is a second possibility: the tree makes its own Revelation. For everything I have said about the Revelation so far could be applied to the tree, as to cairns and songs and other things which are the products of human labour. In the perception of the tree we find the same important here-ness and the now-ness of something-which-is-not-nothing, and a sign that the world is populated by life. The colour of its flowers, the texture of its bark, the fragrance of its pollen, all form part of the tree's identity. All the ways in which it grows and flowers, and every-thing involved in the ways it stays alive, is its assertion of the desirability of life. Its seeds, which is its means of spreading more life into the world, is likewise its assertion of the desir-ability of life.

This idea is artistically represented in The Green Man, which is the image of a man's face emerging from leaves; alternatively his hair, beard, and skin is made of leaves. He's a curious character: sometimes he's depicted scowling, sometimes in serene contemplation, sometimes smiling and laughing. We find him all over the greatest of mediaeval and early modern European cathedrals. His artistic predecessors appear in much earlier buildings, including a few pre-Christian monuments. Art historians sometimes say that he represents the *animus*, the spirit or the intelligence within the plant life of the earth, by which it 'knows' things like how to turn its leaves to the sun, and when to flower and when to seed, and so on. That his image appears on so many of Christendom's most important monuments suggests to me that the builders felt themselves involved in a kind of sacred relationship with their working materials, and with the life of the world around them. They therefore honoured that relationship by giving their working materials a human face. (A stonemason recently taught me that a lot of those Green Men on mediaeval cathedrals bear the faces of the masons who carved them. So they may also serve as a kind of inside joke: the mason's own way of saying "I am here!"). We also find this idea artistically represented in images of the sun and moon with human faces, and depictions of totemic animals. We find it in mythologies that explain various environmental processes like the turning of the seasons as the activities of the gods. The sexual coupling of Dagda and Morrígan, for instance, is an essential symbol in Irish Celtic mythology for the return of fertility to the earth in the spring.

The idea that the world as such makes its own Revelation may seem to stretch the meaning of the word 'assertion'. And it may seem inconsistent with what I wrote earlier of how a message implies a messenger. Some critic might say that only a *person* can assert something, because only a person can have a self-aware *will* to assert something. (Well, there might be some who believe that there *are* persons in trees and animals, but let's leave that aside for now.) To satisfy that critic, I might phrase the assertion in the passive voice: instead of 'the tree is revealing itself', the logical expression might be 'a Revelation is taking place here, in this tree'. That this assertion is driven by natural forces of biology, instead of by conscious intelligence, is perhaps of less importance.

The Revelation of the natural world might be more obvious in the things that animals do. Consider a wolf urinating on a rock to mark its territory: surely this is an assertion of "I am here!", even if only intended for other wolves. Consider bird calls: in the mating season birds sing to attract potential mates. Many birds are also territorial, and will do a daily tour of the area around their nets, stopping in various places to sing a distinctive song which tells other birds "I am here – and this territory belongs to me!" I've seen cardinals fight each other in mid air over the right to perch on a telephone pole and sing that territory-establishing song.

If this still seems unconvincing, another alternative is that there is more than one type of Revelation. The first type, which we have already seen, is the Revelation through conscious and deliberate human labour, such as in music and in architecture. A second type is natural, and takes the form of the activity of living things in an ecosystem. The natural Revelation happens everywhere. All over the earth, living things stretch themselves out, unfold themselves, move, grow, eat, reproduce, excrete, and die, all in pursuit of *more life*. Our own capacity to affirm life might exist on a scale of values, or on a continuum of intensity. That scale runs from the simple, like an apple flower opening to invite a pollinating bee, to the complex, like actors at the Stratford Festival performing Shakespeare's *King Lear*. This would give us a way to see the beauty of both as emerging from a similar impulse in organic life. In the apple tree, this process discharges itself without consciousness of doing so: it is like a song without a singer, yet there is singing happening nonetheless. Perhaps that is what matters most.

§ 31. The Parasite

This exploration of the idea that things in the world make their own Revelations might seem incomplete for another reason. Consider the disease of cancer: there is nothing beautiful about it. Nor is there anything aesthetically compelling about aggressive parasites or viruses, like tapeworms, or herpes. These organisms survive and propagate by attacking, exploiting, and sometimes destroying a host organism. I can't think of anything aesthetically pleasing about that. This is a serious challenge to the thesis that the world makes its own Revelation of the goodness of life.

In reply to this objection, it could be said that a cancerous tumour, or a parasite, or the like, is comparable to the human criminal. Both make their own Revelation of presence, yet both do so in a pathologically disordered kind of way. The virus which destroys its host also destroys itself too. Its alternative is to find a new host to attack, but that only postpones the dilemma, like a kind of holding strategy. The 'successful' parasites in nature eventually cease to be parasites, and evolve into co-dependant organisms which reproduce together with its host. These are called symbiotes, and the process of co-dependant reproduction is called symbiogenesis. You have millions of symbiotes already living within you – they are the mitochondria within each of your cells. They are the descendants of a parasitic attack on our species many millennia ago. They still have their own DNA. And they reproduce with us. They are so intertwined in our biology now that they cannot live without us, nor can we live without them. We see from this example that the will to life, even at the cellular and genetic level, must contain no internal contradiction.

We can also see how beauty emerges from a life-affirming *response* to the ugliness of things like terminal diseases. I have a friend whose mother recently died of breast cancer. It was truly beautiful to see the solidarity and support shown by her family and close friends, and her own will to fight the disease and preserve her dignity as long as possible. She dealt with her situation by affirming her life. But I think that does not retroactively sanctify the disease that was its impetus. Cancer is not rendered good and beautiful just because some people respond to it with courage and determination. I'm quite sure that the gods didn't create viral parasites in order to teach us to be persevering and compassionate.

Having said all that, it remains important to remember that the Revelation of the goodness and beauty of life is only partly an observation about the world. It is also partly an act of will. A Revelation against loneliness must presuppose the ethical desirability of life on earth as a first-order proposition, even as the world is also full of deep-down torrents and crimson seas. This presupposition gains strength from the discovery of beauty in the world around. Indeed the evidence of the beauty of the life of the world makes it *rational* to say Yes to life in the way that the Revelation must do. For the Revelation of the world supports, sustains, encourages, and harmonizes well with the Revelation of a non-disordered human will. But the quelling of loneliness, paradoxical as it may seem, must begin inside one's own being. One must look within, and put one's own ship in order, before venturing to the waterfront of the world. As the Charge of the Goddess teaches, "If you cannot find it within, you will never find it without".

§ 32. The Razor's Edge

We have looked at the case for the ethical desirability of life from several angles now. I've shown how other programs of value, like criminal violence, lead to self-refuting ends. With the help of Aristotle and Kant I've tried to show that the ethical desirability of life is already logically presupposed in everything else we do. With Clark and Schweitzer I've tried to show that it is also involved in the idea civilisation itself. We've also seen how it appears in the world of nature. I've given all this time to this part of the Revelation because I think it is the most important part. If I may use the words of Martin Luther as a precedent: it is here, at the third movement of the Revelation, that we must take a stand. When the existential loneliness of being is confronted directly, we have to set aside relativism, the clichés of pop culture, and any lingering flappery. For it is here, perhaps more than anywhere else, that worthwhile and meaningful and *spiritual* lives are made.

There is a kind of tension between Loneliness and Revelation, between being and non-being, between life-affirmation and angst-ridden despair. *Both*, it seems to me, are original situations; both are existential conditions of life. Between the emptiness of interstellar space, and the lusciousness of the green and living earth, human life stands, as on the edge of a razor. Which of them takes precedence over the other is partly something we can observe in the world, and partly something we must resolve within ourselves. The quality and the worth of one's own life may depend greatly upon this resolution. For a person can be no good to himself or to others unless he systematically assumes that it is good to be alive, good to be human, good to be who he is. If he believes otherwise, it may as well be said of him that he is a zombie. For his body is only going through the motions of life, and the spirit is long since gone.

Thus the logic that is in play here is only partly a matter of

Kantian will, or Aristotelian virtue, or historical observation. It is also a logic of an ethical-aesthetic dialogue between the individual and the things and people of world she meets and is related to. This dialogue is governed by the *creative and moral necessity to affirm the goodness and beauty of life*. The person who asserts that proposition then acts as if it is true, and in so doing, *makes it true*. This is to suggest, perhaps, that a moral principle, the ethical desirability of life, can be a creative force in the world.

Loneliness is an amazing thing. Yet I hope that some confidence in life can be instilled with the thought that the intelligent mind which is able to grasp and *understand* this cosmic loneliness, is perhaps equally amazing! The mind which fully understands that she is but a tiny grain of dust in the cosmic bottomless vastness of the universe *still finds that she is something-that-is-not-nothing*. The mere fact that I can contemplate this existential loneliness shows me that my life is worth something, at least as a thinker, if not as anything more. And while that something may well be very small, the intellectual power to contemplate an immensity is just as astonishing as the immensity which is the object of that contemplation. Wherever you can see, hear, and comprehend things, so can your spirit dwell. Thus the thinking mind which finds itself beset with a hope-crushing isolation can also discover, paradoxically, *within* that same isolation, confidence enough to inspire hope.

Yet this discovery is only partly an observation. It is also an act of will. It falls to us, as human beings and as would-be *spiritual* beings, to find, to create, and to invent a way to affirm the desirability of life. The ethical moment of the Revelation is a deliberately chosen act of life, an act of undaunted magnificent life, which emerges from the very loneliness that seems to preclude it. Here all notions of relativism, as attractive as they may seem, must be set aside. Here we choose not just for ourselves, but for all beings. Here we stand; we cannot do otherwise.

§ 33. The Mist

There might be other conclusions that could be drawn from the proposition that life makes its own Revelation. There might be a God or two at work in the world, showing themselves to us as shadows in the mist of a Celtic twilight. There might be many spiritual beings dwelling in the world, giving us gifts and showing us love all the time. I don't know this; nor do I not know this. I only know what I can sense with the organs of my body, what I can do with the work of my hands, what I can say with my voice, and what I can contemplate with the fire in my mind. Everything else is probably speculation.

§ 34. The Vision

What if the Revelation of the life of the world is not existential, but transcendental? What if the beauty of things emerges not from the way things are in the world, but from something that precedes, or supercedes, embodied existence: an essence, a higher reality, a cosmic order, a Platonic Form, even a god? A columnist in my local newspaper recounted this idea:

> Stand on the shore of any lake, look up at the clear sky and see that we are part of this immense wonder of everything. If we cannot see, we can still sense this connection. By recognizing this connection, we come closer to an understanding of God or whatever term you may wish to use to describe this connection. (Louis Spizzirri, as cited by Barrie Hopkins, "Bits and Pieces" *The Wellington Advertiser*, 19th June 2009.)

The writer also noted that we do not need organized religious institutions, or dogmas, or "a priest, a rabbi, a shaman or anyone else" to procure this understanding, although "if you need someone to guide and direct you, that's okay". I've chosen to cite a newspaper letter instead of a philosophical text to show that this is probably a widespread idea, and that it can occur to anyone in any walk of life. This idea might be a way to avoid some of the problems just mentioned, while at the same time avoiding the traps of nihilism and loneliness. Still, this proposition carries its own series of problems, some of which have already been noted. The gods might be human psychological projections on to the cosmos, and thus only fantasies. Or, if they do exist, they might be astonishingly lonely, far more so than you and I. But perhaps for that very reason, they too feel a need to reveal themselves. Therefore they make the trees and sunsets and other wonders of the world their Revelations of presence.

The Greek philosopher Plato, who lived from 427 to 347 BCE, believed that goodness is an immaterial and impersonal *eidos* (idea, or form) which is eternal, and which transcends the embodied world. He also appears to have believed that it has some kind of creative role in the world. His explanation appears in the famous Analogy of the Sun: "What the good itself is in the intelligible realm, in relation to understanding and intelligible things, the sun is in the visible realm, in relation to sight and visible things." (*Republic*, 508b) In that passage he is claiming that our knowledge of good things in the worlds depends on our knowledge of the 'eidos' (form, idea, intellectual-being) of goodness itself, just in the same way that our ability to see things in the world depends on the light of the sun. As this analogy continues, he includes something very curious:

> You'll be willing to say, I think, that the sun not only provides visible things with the power to be seen but also with coming to be, growth, and nourishment... Therefore, you should also say that not only do the objects of knowledge owe their being known to the good, but their being is also due to it, although the good is not being, but superior to it in rank and power. (*Republic*, 509b)

Plato's argument is a little weird, I must admit. On the surface it appears he is saying that the Form of *to agathon*, 'the beautiful good', in-forms good things in the world, and is in some way responsible for the existence of good things. By analogy, just as the sun shines on things, and helps the plants to grow, so too does the Form of The Beautiful Good encourage the coming-to-be of good and beautiful things. The idea of goodness is thus not just one more material property of things, like something's being tall, or being red. Rather, *to agathon* is somehow involved in the way things are. An argument like this, if true, could support the proposition that beautiful things in the world make their own Revelation. What we see in the beautiful apple tree is the Form of the Good, revealing itself through the tree.

Some six centuries or more later, the philosopher Plotinus (205-270 CE) studied the works of Plato in the famous Library of Alexandria. Building on Plato's theory of forms, Plotinus claims that Beauty is a property of that which is a unified, self-contained totality. But only the Forms can be self-contained totalities. For nothing in the visible, mortal world 'has' itself so completely as the Forms do. Only the Forms, therefore, are beautiful; and any beautiful thing in the world owes its beauty to the way it is *in-formed* by the Forms. To further demonstrate his point: Plotinus invites the reader to:

> ...make a mental picture of our universe: each member shall remain what it is, distinctly apart, yet all is to form, as far as possible, a complete unity so that whatever comes into view, say the outer orb of the heavens, shall bring immediately with it the vision, on the one plane, of the sun and all the stars with earth and sea and all living things as if exhibited upon a transparent globe. (Plotinus, *Ennead*, V.8.9)

Only this totality, says Plotinus, has true Being; only this holistic vision of the universe truly *is*. Therefore, he says, only this totality is beautiful. It's not quite right to say that in Plotinus' vision, beauty is a property of the totality of Being. Rather, it's the case that in the totality, Being and Beauty merge into a single concept, a single intellectual understanding, and become one and the same. In his words:

> Beauty without Being could not be, nor Being voided of beauty; abandoned of Beauty, Being loses something of its essence. Being is desirable because it is identical with Beauty; and Beauty is loved because it is Being. How then can we

debate which is the cause of the other, where the nature is one? (*ibid.*)

This text is a mouthful of strange-sounding logic, but the idea expressed here is fairly simple. The apple tree is beautiful because it somehow participates or shares in the greater Beauty of the totality of Being. This is a further elaboration of the Platonic view that *to agathon* has some kind of responsibility for the way things are in the world. And this vision informs many of the ideas that mystics and occultists both east and west have of ecstatic unity with God, with enlightenment and release. Plotinus' student and main biographer, Porphyry, said that he personally observed Plotinus achieve an enlightened state of consciousness by means of this meditation four times.

I think the vision of Plotinus, and the neo-Platonic tradition he created, is magnificent. I cannot help but be amazed by it, and amazed by the intellectual and imaginative powers of those philosophers who bequeathed it to us. However, I also find it very troubling too. The Revelation of the beauty of the world does not emerge from mystical visions of higher planes of reality. The Revelation is an embodied presence, here and now. Similarly our ethical principles do not emerge from transcendental abstractions. Rather, these things emerge from the thick of the embodied world, even with all its problems, its miseries and complications, and all its lonely nights. Mystical visions of higher spiritual realities call for the preceptor to turn his mind precisely *away* from the mortal realm, away from the very place where we live and where we have all our experiences, and where our ethical principles matter most. I recognise that visions of global inter-connectedness and cosmic unity are capable of inspiring important ethical ideas like universal compassion and peace. This is part of the message of the great religions of the East, like Hinduism and Buddhism, and mystical forms of Islam such as Sufism. In fact this idea is prominent in the New Age movement too. Yet the unity of the world and the presence of the divine is not a commandment to be obeyed. For the universe does not teach anything: the universe just *is*. The unity of the world and the presence of the divine is *a question to be answered and a problem to be resolved*. Ethical ideas like universal compassion emerge not from the divine vision itself but from *the human response to the vision,* and from the human interpretation of that vision. We may well belong to a global and cosmic togetherness: but the ethical significance of that membership is a product of our own thinking and our own dialogue with the other people who share it.

§ 35. The Message

If a transcendental understanding of beauty like this one is true, nonetheless it still falls to us to decide what to do about it. Whether the Revelation of the beautiful tree emerges from its way of being in the world, or from a transcendental form in which it participates, it doesn't follow that we will automatically know how to live. There's nothing in what I've said so far that suggests anything like a moral duty to respect or to cherish the tree, the river, or the Earth as a whole, *just because* it happens to offer a Revelation like this. The apple tree presents itself to us as the bearer of the implicit presence of the higher world: but its message is *not* 'Do this, don't do that, can't you read the sign?'

Let me be even more controversial, and say it is the same for the gods themselves. It is the same for Krishna, Yahweh, Sophia, Morrígan, Odin, Queen Isis, Baron Samedi, and the Jade Emperor. It is the same for all the heroes, ancestors, spirits, saints, and prophets too. And it is the same for impersonal sacred powers, like the Hindu Atman, the Buddha Nature, the 'Light' of the new age, and the Druidic Awen. *Their mere presence is their message.* If that message had to be put into words, it would go like this: 'I am here, and this is who I am, and what I am is beautiful.'

Furthermore I suspect that is their *only* message. Everything else is our own interpretation. The sacred teachings of all the gods: the Peace of the Morrígan, the Precepts of Delphi, the Ten Commandments, the Gospels, the Seven Pillars of Islam, the Four Noble Truths, the Vedas and Upanisads, are all the works of people. Each of these texts is a different way of trying to understand, express, narrate, come to grips with, respond to, and deal with that divine message. It is the same for the stories, legends, and mythologies that we tell of our religious heroes. This is true even if those heroes are not fictitious characters but were once living human beings. The stories of their lives, as they were told, re-told, changed, edited, exaggerated, and preserved over time, are but products of a human attempt to understand the divine Revelation. But the Revelation, in itself and on its own, does not tell us what to do. It is a presence to be experienced, not a commandment to be obeyed.

Yet that may be not so bad after all. This thesis suggests that the gods that we praise and the way we praise them reveals as much about ourselves as it does about the gods. That kind of knowledge strikes me as very enlightening. It also leaves all decisions and the power of initiative in our own hands. For any given problem or situation, the message of the gods is always the same. First they reveal their presence: "I am here" Then they reveal something of their identity: "This is what I am". Then they reveal something of the beauty and goodness of the part of the world in which they are involved. "What I am is beautiful!". That message cannot be used to justify any kind of political program. It cannot justify class divisions, economic disparity, warfare, oppression, racism, sexism, or acts of religiously motivated terrorism. The gods tell us that they are here, but they do not tell us what to do. We have to make our own decisions. Whatever deity you praise, perhaps she can help give you hope and encouragement and energy, but then you have to use that energy on your own. I find this a very life-affirming and empowering prospect.

§ 36. "Is Anyone Else Out There?"

By building your inukshuk, you see the effect of your labour on the world and thus you know you exist. But knowledge of one's own existence alone cannot stave off loneliness. Indeed under some circumstances, a Revelation intended only for yourself can *heighten* your loneliness. One who is conscious of his existence soon becomes conscious of the solitude of existence. The quelling of loneliness requires a second. Thus the implicit 'I am here' within every assertion of presence also carries an implicit question: *'Is anyone else out there?'*

A Revelation can thus be compared to a lighthouse that guides lost ships to the harbour. Its purpose is not only to establish the presence of its builder. Its purpose is also to search for other beings who could acknowledge that presence. Only a being capable of asserting its own presence can make that acknowledgement, for only such a being knows what it is to assert presence. For that reason, the Revelation becomes *a search for other presences*, and a seeking-out of other Revelations in the world.

As with the assertion of 'I am here!', the question 'Is anyone out there?', may not be on the forefront of a singer's mind. She already knows one possible answer to that question, for she already knows at least one being in the world who can acknowledge her creation: herself. The artist can always be her own audience. In this sense, the question is always answered immediately. But that answer can only give temporary satisfaction. It takes a second presence, the presence of one who is *not yourself*, to acknowledge one's own presence in a way that will stave off loneliness with any success.

There are several good examples of this from literature. In the second act of Beckett's play *Waiting for Godot*, the messenger-boy from Godot appears for the second time. Although he is clearly the same boy from the first act, he claims not to recognise the two hobos Vladimir and Estragon. Indeed at first the boy addresses Vladimir with the wrong name. Just before he leaves, Vladimir asks him to give this message to Mr. Godot:

"Tell him – tell him you saw me and that – tell him that you saw me. You're sure you saw me, you won't come and tell me tomorrow that you never saw me!"
(Beckett, *Waiting for Godot*. Pg. 92)

Vladimir is a man with not many particulars about him: he has no home or family or job or even much of a personal history. His identity has been reduced, as if it was subject to Husserl's *epoché*. But the one desperate need that he certainly does possess, which cannot be stripped away from him, is the need to be seen and remembered by another human being. If he is not seen and remembered, he might as well not exist. It is for this reason, primarily, that Vladimir and his equally nondescript friend Estragon cannot leave each other, even when they declare the intention to do so. The company of someone who frustrates and annoys him is better than no company at all.

There are examples from history too. Prisoners at the Nazi labour camp of Auschwitz, as many historical accounts affirm, were essentially stripped of their identities and particulars. More than a million people were sent there, and put to work as slaves, until they died from exhaustion, or disease, or were murdered. Recently, however, archaeologists found a message written by seven of the prisoners. It was found on a piece of paper in a bottle, buried in the wall of a nearby building that the prisoners had been compelled to repair. The message contains nothing more than the names, home towns, and prison numbers of seven people, most of them from Poland, and all of them between the ages of 18 and 20. Museum interpreters said that the authors "were young people who were trying to leave some trace of their existence behind them". ("Builders find Auschwitz message" *BBC News*, 27th April 2009; Ryan Lucas, 'Workmen in Poland find hidden Auschwitz message" *The Washington Post / The Associated Press*, 27th April 2009.) Examples like these suggest the one last wish that can remain in a person, when everything else has been taken away, including his very human dignity, is the wish to be known and remembered.

In this way, a Revelation is an embodiment of its maker's loneliness. It reveals not only its maker's presence and way of being in the world, but also the extent of its maker's solitude. Corresponding to each Revelation that someone may create, there is an explicit seeking of, or an implicit hope for, other people. That which cannot be permanently suspended in anyone, so long as she is alive, is the will to establish her presence on earth, the will to assert herself as something-that-is-not-nothing, and especially the wish to be seen, heard, known, and remembered. This wish resides deep within each of us. It is sometimes stronger than the wish to be loved. It can remain strong even in people who live in the very worst of circumstances, and who have no expectation of survival. It is fulfilled when the cairn-builder finds that someone added a stone to his monument, or built her own cairn nearby. It is fulfilled when others applaud her song, or sing along with her, or sing their own song in response. It is fulfilled when someone finds a way to say, 'I saw that cairn you built; I heard the song you sang; I found something of you in the world, and thus I knew and remembered you.'

§ 37. The Musician

Music and the spoken word exemplifies this fourth moment of Revelation which is also true of architecture but is harder to discern there. One who sings a song or plays an instrument, sings or plays *for* someone. Especially in music, the Word of Being is spoken *in the hope of hearing an answering call from another being*. Thus the Revelation in music asserts the statement 'I am here!', and at the same time asserts the question: 'Is anyone else out there?'

For a Revelation offered to a void says only half, perhaps less than half, of all that can be said. The assertion of presence is the means by which a being asserts herself as something rather than nothing. But without the answering word from another being, acknowledging that Revelation, doubts may linger, and through that doubt loneliness may enter.

This is partly true of architecture also: buildings have purposes, inhabitants, visitors, and sometimes admirers. But the architect may have his audience at any time after the building is complete. The architect can sleep soundly knowing his creation will probably last for a while, and that if he doesn't have an audience today, he may have one tomorrow. When we, thousands of years later, find his cairn on the Arctic plain or the Connemara field, we become his audience. One who contemplates architecture may read the presence of people in the past, if not in the present. The cairn tells us that once upon a time, people lived here.

The musician, by contrast, knows her song will last no longer than the performance itself. She must have an audience in the here and now, or else she will have no audience at all. One who contemplates live music knows that someone is here, right now. Live music is always absolutely unique to the occasion in which it is performed. No live performance of some song is exactly the same as another performance of the same song, even if performed by the same musicians. In some way, whether large or small, things will have changed. There may be inflections in the voice, or different twitches in the fingers that hold the instruments, different pauses between breaths, and different dramatic emphasis or timing on various measures. A similar point can be made about actors in live theatre, as well as dancers and other performing artists. Recorded music, because it is produced in its moment by a machine, and not by a person, is not the same as live music. Machine-produced sounds can signify that once upon a time, someone somewhere sang that song. In terms of its Revelation, recorded music is more like a cairn. But live music, live theater and live dance performances are inherently time-bounded. They cannot outlast the moment unless they are lodged in the memory of an audience. They therefore seek that audience, perhaps more desperately than architecture does.

Someone may object by saying that she is no less a performer when she sings in the shower by herself. But in this case, the singer becomes her own audience. Music is no less a performative art when the same person is both performer and listener. The singer asserts her own presence to herself. But that seems to do only half of what needs to be done. Consider what it would be like to compose and perform the most wonderful music in the world without ever hearing a note of it, nor ever hearing a word of response from a listener. This was the case for Ludwig van Beethoven. Around the year 1796, when he was about twenty-five years old, he began to experience tinnitus, a debilitating ringing in his ears which would slowly yet inexorably destroy his hearing. By 1806 his hearing was almost entirely gone, and his doctors told him there was no hope for its return or restoration. In the Austrian town of Heiligenstadt, where he was living at the time, he wrote a letter to his friends and family that expressed his exquisite emotional turmoil and isolation. The letter has come to be known as the Heiligenstadt Testament. It reads, in part:

> Reflect now that for six years I have been a hopeless case, aggravated by senseless physicians, cheated year after year in the hope of improvement, finally compelled to face the prospect of a lasting malady (whose cure will take years or, perhaps, be impossible), born with an ardent and lively temperament, even susceptible to the diversions of society, I was compelled early to isolate myself, to live in loneliness, when I at times tried to forget all this. O how harshly was I repulsed by the doubly sad experience of my bad hearing, and yet it was impossible for me to say to men "speak louder, shout, for I am deaf". Ah how could I possibly admit such an infirmity in the one sense which should have been more perfect in me than in others, a sense which I once possessed in highest perfection, a perfection such as few surely in my profession enjoy or have enjoyed - O I cannot do it, therefore forgive me when you see me draw back when I would gladly mingle with you... (cited in Lockwood, *Beethoven: The Music and the Life*)

As you can see, this is a letter written by a man whose heart was utterly broken. When he wrote this letter, he was already well known at that time as a genius composer and pianist. He was also already known for his impatience, perfectionism, gruffness, moodiness, and demanding character. By all accounts, he was very difficult to deal with. Yet his letter exposes his deepest heart's feelings: he reveals himself as very self-aware, yet emotionally fragile, vulnerable, and profoundly lonely. To him, the loss of his hearing was the loss of his entire world. It cut him off from the things he loved most, and marooned him inside his own mind. So ashamed was he about his condition that he never delivered this letter. It was found after his death, hidden in his desk drawer, some twenty-five years after it was written.

Furthermore, the letter also reveals that the loneliness brought on by his disability very nearly drove him to suicide. It is said that his hearing eventually became so acutely bad that when his famous Ninth Symphony was performed for the first time, on the 7th of May 1824, he could not hear the audience's applause at all. He began to weep openly, believing that everyone hated his music. The contralto had to stand up and physically turn him around. Then he saw that the audience was in fact on their feet, waving their hands, throwing their hats in the air, overjoyed with the glorious music he had given them. Even that, however, only temporarily lifted his spirits. The following day, his friends told him how the whole city was talking about his symphony and singing as many of its melodies as they could remember. Beethoven's downcast response was that the performance made him very little money.

Architecture can create to last. Its medium is solid matter: wood, stone, metal, clay, glass, plastic, concrete, and so on. Architecture can have its audience many years or centuries after everyone involved in its construction has passed away. Music, by contrast, has the immaterial force of sound for its medium. It is inherently transient; it requires its audience immediately. Architecture can assert the builder's presence apparently forever – or at least until the building is destroyed or let fall to ruin. Music asserts the singer's presence only in its own moment. It cannot hold back the frontier of loneliness any longer than that. It needs is acknowledgement that *someone was listening* in the same here-and-now moment. Without that acknowledgement, the song dies on the singer's lips, and then the loneliness that the song pushed back is given space to rush in again.

§ 38. The Camp Fire

Someone who finds a cairn built along her path knows that others have gone before her this way, and that others may perhaps not be far off. A cairn on the ridge tells us, besides whatever else it may tell us, that the world is a *populated* world. This can be a comforting thought. Yet it is not, I'm almost sorry to say, a full and complete solution to the problem of loneliness. The sight of the cairn in the stone field, the sound of a song in the distance, may serve as a resting place, where thoughts of solitude may be put away for a while. But once the song ends, and once we get walking again and leave the cairn behind, loneliness has a chance to find us again. Similarly, someone who builds a cairn or sings a song may still find loneliness shrouding her. For the making of one's own Revelation does not by itself put an end to loneliness.

What it does do, however, is *push the frontier of loneliness away for a while*. When we reveal ourselves to each other, we reduce the loneliness of existence, and replace it, in great or small ways, with the assertion of presence, identity, and of will to affirm the goodness and beauty of life. The first and second movements in the process of banishing loneliness are the activities involved in seeing others as they really are, and showing yourself to others as you really are. This initial act of Revelation, in which people *reveal* themselves to each other, has some logical priority over any other particular 'modality' of relation. It comes before friendship, respect, appreciation, and sharing; it comes before criticism and judgement; it even comes before love. The Revelation is the *foundation* of all those things. It makes them possible. In any mature and sound relationship, no matter what its nature, there is first an act of seeing and being seen, and hearing and being heard.

The third moment of the Revelation is the moment when the

acts of seeing and being seen take on ethical significance. But it is the fourth moment, the search for others, which can do the most to push back the frontier of loneliness. For loneliness cannot be banished by just making one's presence merely known to others somehow. Nor is it eliminated by forgetting oneself in the presence of others. The quelling of loneliness requires a second. And as noted earlier, anyone else who the lonely heart turns to is usually absorbed in her own problems. Thus, the conundrum is that no one rescues herself from loneliness, and no one rescues anyone else from loneliness. But *people working together may collaboratively release each other from loneliness*. This they may do when they approach each other from a place within themselves where they both found and created a desire for life, and a desire for the goodness of life. Then, having met each other, they create a shared way of being in the world.

I think this is the most honest and direct way to meet the problem of loneliness. When people help each other face loneliness, they push the frontiers of loneliness back further than one person alone can do. Think of a campfire at night. A campfire creates a circle of warmth and light around it, which can be large or small, as the fire itself is large or small. Within the circle of the firelight, people can see each other, and be seen by each other. They can cook food together, and stay warm together, and do things together. A life-affirming way of being in the world is like that campfire. Someone who enters its circle of light and warmth finds that she may feel at home, feel safe while at rest, and feel, at long last, as if she truly belongs exactly where she is.

A shared way of being in the world is like a campfire where many people provide the wood and fuel, and many people eat from the food cooked over its flames. It opens the path to human and environmental relationships, and illuminates the spiritual importance of relationships. Everyone benefits from the warmth and the light of the fire in accord with how much they contribute to its maintenance. Moreover, a shared understanding of what is good for the fire comes into play here. If too much fuel is given to the fire, it burns too hot and too quickly. If too little fuel is given, it burns too cold. If it is given the wrong fuel, it might not burn at all. Similarly, a shared understanding of how we best involve ourselves in each other's lives comes into play. People can give too much or too little, take too much or to little, or give and take the wrong kind of things, and in each case disturb the relationships in which everyone is involved. But as people get to know each other, they learn what is good for the fire that warms and feeds them all, which is to learn what is good for each other and for the relationships in which they are involved. In that way, they can banish loneliness more completely than anyone can do on their own.

When I speak of a shared way of being in the world, I do not mean merely having interests in common with other people. Nor do I speak of merely having similar purposes, nor 'filling in' what is 'missing' in each other. The language of economics simply will not do. Rather, what I have in mind is the transformation of the first movement of the Revelation from the singular to the plural: from 'I' to 'We'.

§ 39. The Harbour

This fourth moment of the Revelation is another place where ethical ideas play a role. The place for the ethical was already prepared in previous meditations, when the Revelation-maker had to assert the ethical desirability of life in a consistent and confident way. Here, too, in the search for others, decisions have to be made, and values acknowledged. In this process, let us recall the *epoché*, as a philosophical method for discerning the essence of things. Any transient, utilitarian, or temporary elements are noted and put aside, so that we can arrive at something essential. Thus the ethical ideas in the Revelation, if there are any, cannot be accidental. One way to do this is to examine and reject reasons for entering into relationships which are transient and temporary. Aristotle, back in the 5ᵗʰ century BCE, did something like this when he observed that friendships based on utility or practical expediency normally don't last very long. In his words:

> These friendships are based on an accident, since the friend is not loved for being what he is, but as affording some benefit or pleasure as the case may be. Consequently, friendships of this kind are easily broken off, in the event of the parties themselves changing, for if no longer pleasant or useful to each other, they cease to love each other. (*NE* 8.iii.3)

Aristotle's argument suggests that when there is a change in the practical purposes which brought people together as friends, then the people usually part ways. It follows, so he says, that such transient friendships are not true friendships. If a friendship is to last, it must be based on something which could survive such changes. In a similar manner, consider the words of the 20ᵗʰ century philosopher Martin Buber:

Whoever says You does not have something for his object. For wherever there is something there is also another something: every It borders on other Its; It is only by virtue of bordering on others. But where You is said there is no something. You has no borders. Whoever says You does not have something; he has nothing. But he stands in relation. (Buber, *I and Thou*, pg. 55)

The point which I think is common in Aristotle and Buber is that some relationships embody certain moral and philosophical principals, and others do not. Aristotle's point is that real friends are not utilitarian possessions: if they were, they would be too shallow and transient. Buber similarly observes that the language of property-possession does not belong to the world of relationships. People cannot be 'possessed' like mere 'things'. This is what is intended by Buber's statement that whoever addresses another with the language of human acknowledgement (that is, with the word 'You') does not *have* something. The very notion of a human relationship thus excludes certain materialistic principles, like property ownership. This is not to say that friends cannot or do not benefit each other materially. But it is to say that the material benefit they provide each other is not the sole reason for the friendship. Something else is also at work here, to keep the people together.

I think the something else which is at work here is a value which we have already seen: the affirmation of the ethical desirability of life. Here, in the third movement of Revelation, this principle is transformed into the ethical desirability of relationships. When we approach other people *as people*, and not as objects to be possessed, as Buber suggests, then we are also at the same time implicitly asserting the goodness of approaching others that way. There is a hint of justice involved: for we implicitly assert that the other person *deserves* to be approached as a person and not as a possession. (One of the traditional understandings of justice is the activity of giving to people what they deserve, whatever that might be.) Further, when we approach others as people and not as possessions, the Revelation of presence that we offer them becomes an invitation to comment, to praise, to criticise, to compete, or to cooperate in the production of another Revelation. We invite other people to become involved in our lives, and we offer to involve ourselves in their lives. In this invitation and offering, one affirms the desirability of one's own life and the life of other people with whom one's own life is variously entangled.

Imagine a ship coming into harbour. How good is the helmsman? Can he plot the stars, shoot the sun, assess the winds and the currents, and get the ship on course to its destination? Can he weather the storms without going too far off course, and without sinking? Piloting and navigating a ship is an ancient symbol for being in the world in a certain way, living a certain kind of life, making hard decisions and practicing various moral qualities. Can the values that you have chosen to live by help you sail your ship well? Similarly, the many ways we relate to others must pass a similar test: approaching a friend is like approaching a harbour on his waterfront. Can you steer your ship to a good landing? Or, will you be caught in a current, smashed on the rocks, or blown out to sea again? Although some of these values must be categorical, such as the wrongness of terrorist killing, others can be more flexible. Just as the goddess Isis revealed herself to Lucius Apulius with many different names, so there can be more than one ethically significant way of being in the world. There doesn't have to be only one true way; there can be many true ways. Yet any way of being in the world must pass the test of life-affirmation. In general, the values which are needed to create, sustain, and uplift our *relationships* are the values which successfully pass through the gateway of the Revelation.

I meet someone new for the first time. I might ask myself: what can I gain from you? How can you benefit me? What do I have to give you in order to get something better back from you? When I am done with you, how do I get rid of you? If these are my questions, then I have not approached you through the gateway; I have not seen you as a human being. If these questions are a major part of my way of being in the world, I will eventually consign myself to the misery, frustration, and fear of an unhappy lonely life. But if I do approach you as a human being, with a world and a mystery and a Revelation of your own, then my questions become: Who are you, and who am I? Do I know who you are? Do you know who I am? Do we see each other clearly? For if we do, and if we take time to look closer and see the Revelation, we can enter into conversations, dialogues, and relationships with each other. And eventually we can create a shared way of being in the world. When we treat people *as people*, we implicitly affirm the goodness of relationships, which is another way of affirming the goodness of life.

These values do not take the form of rules and laws. For the Revelation of the sacred is not a commandment to be obeyed. It is a presence to be experienced. I cannot repeat this little truth often enough. But in the absence of explicit rules and laws, there still is an ethical understanding. Some values support the activities that go into the making of a complete Revelation, and others do not. Some kinds of habits and choices are exemplary of excellence in a revealed presence, and others are not. Some values are admitted with enthusiasm, and some with caution; some are rejected but only conditionally, and some are rejected absolutely. Values like wonder, humanity, and integrity can pass the test easily and clearly. Values like hubris, greed, and resentment probably can't. As already noted, nihilism and misanthropy and murder certainly can't. For most of our decisions, all we will need is a straightforward list of the virtues that one needs, and cannot do without, in order to reveal the goodness of life. One may also need a list of vices which effectively prevent that Revelation. And for this purpose, there are many cards we could pull. We could choose the Heroic virtues (courage, generosity, friendship), or the Classical virtues (courage, temperance, prudence, justice), or the Seven Grandfathers (Wisdom, Truth, Humility, Bravery, Honesty, Love, and Respect), or the Christian virtues (which are the same as the classical virtues, but with the addition of faith, hope, and charity). It could be almost any similar list, in accord with what makes the most sense in the time and place where you live, and the kinds of relationships in which you are involved. But whatever they are, they have to help you sail your ship well, safely reach whatever harbour you approach, and perhaps also sail your ship in formation with hers, without colliding, or drifting apart. They have to help us create *shared* ways of being in the world, and shared Revelations: they must be able to transform the 'I' of the 'I am here!' into 'We'.

§ 40. The Lovers' Gaze

A practical way to explain how the 'I' of the Revelation is transformed into 'We' is to use the example of falling in love. I can only describe it from my own experience, although I do hope, dear reader, that my experience is not especially different from yours. So let me begin by doing something that most everyone does: walk along a public street. Let us suppose that I am on my way to present a public lecture. (That is how I make my livelihood, after all). As I walk I think of many things which have nothing to do with love. I might rehearse the speech in my mind, or I might wonder how many people will attend, or I might wonder what the weather will be tomorrow. As I walk, other people pass me by, and for the most part I ignore them. But I might take notice of one or two out of every hundred. Here's a woman who resembles a well-known actress. There's a man who seems in an unusual rush. Here's a child playing with the same kind of toy that I once played with as a child. I notice those who *stand out* for whatever reason. Someone might stand out because she possesses some of the features that might typically be called 'beautiful', or which popular culture presents to us as 'ideal'. She might have a slim waist, or an up-to-date sense of fashion. Or, she might stand out because she has bad teeth, for instance. But for whatever reason, she is *noticeable*. This is not the same as falling in love with someone. But it is an essential moment, an initial condition without which falling in love cannot happen.

I arrive at the venue for my lecture. The host introduces me, I open my notes and begin to speak. As I do, I also read my audience. Can everyone hear me clearly enough? Are people interested in my talk, or are they bored? Again, my thoughts are on anything but love. Someone sitting just to my left has thick and curly red hair, and fair skin, and bright eyes. I notice this. And then I notice that she is noticing me. She is listening to my talk like everyone else, but she is also attending to my posture, the movements of my hands, the inflection of my voice, and perhaps a number of other things that have little to do with how I am playing the role of a public speaker. This is where the process of falling in love truly begins. I notice someone, and at the same time she notices me. I also notice that she noticed me, and she noticed that I noticed her. A dozen people might have noticed me as I walked to the tree-lined grove where my lecture is set, and for whatever reason I ignored almost all of them. But this time I notice someone at the same time that she notices me. This is a magical moment. It is the first communication between two people who might fall in love with each other, and who may indeed be deciding whether to allow themselves to fall.

This mutual notice is the first moment of the fall into love, but it is not love itself. Although it is part of love, it is only a small fraction of love. The next thing that happens is that I try to make myself *more noticeable*, and not by just anyone, but by *her*. I look in her direction more often, and I smile more when I look her way. When I take questions from the audience, I find myself hoping that *she* will be impressed by my answers. She tries to make herself more noticeable by me, too, by making an unusual comment, or just by throwing her hair over her shoulder in a way that makes me forget what I'm doing for a second. At the end of the lecture, people come forward to ask more questions, or suggest further research for me, or even to continue a friendly debate. Still, my mind is distracted. It's amazing how the initial stages of falling in love resemble a hypnotic trance. One by one people leave, as they finish their brief conversation with me, and find other things to do. One by one they go, until she and I are the only two remaining. I sit next to her, I ask silly questions about what she thought of the lecture, and how far she traveled to be here. She asks me what inspired the ideas I spoke of today, and how long it took to prepare them. Somewhere among the "polite meaningless phrases", we look into each other's eyes, and then we say no more.

Eye contact is very psychologically powerful. This is not the gaze that Sartre wrote of, which transforms everything it sees into an object, potentially to be used and possessed (and disposed of). As Lévinas wrote, the Other who gazes upon you is obviously not a 'thing' among other things of the world. The Other is a person, distinct and autonomous, and as a person she cannot be owned. Thus, according to Lévinas, the gaze "commands justice" and precludes violence. There is simply no doing harm to someone who asserts her presence and identity as a human being, with her own feelings and her own autonomy. That is unless, of course, we first suppress within ourselves the humanity that the gaze evokes in us. Yet it is also in the gaze, especially the silent gaze, when love has its first genesis. Mythology provides excellent examples of this. It was the first gaze between Guinevere and Lancelot which ignited the love between them. The illicit love between Tristan and Isolde is first explained as the effect of a magic potion. But their feeling for each other truly began when they met each other in the eye, once the potion was drunk and they realised what they had done. These mythologies speak of the psychological force of the gaze, the meeting of the eyes. I think the gaze is powerful because it enables people to see into each other's minds. By this I do not mean anything psychic or telepathic. It's the little movements of the face, and especially the eye, not governed by the conscious rational will, which show what's going on within. In the mode of a biological reflex, they spontaneously reflect whatever thoughts and impulses and feelings dwell beneath the surface. (Consider the way most people's eyes dart to the left, just for a fraction of a second, whenever they tell a lie.) The gaze from eye to eye focuses itself on those little movements. It ignores the public roles we play in order to fulfill the duties of a job, or keep up the appearance that all is well. It dispels the illusions and penetrates the disguises we don to protect our true selves. It focuses instead on the human presence: the person, the individual, the human being, with all her quirks and interests, attractions and aversions, habits and foibles. With most or all of the public superficialities penetrated, all that remains is the pure presence, the "I am here," of the Revelation. This human presence cannot be faked or suppressed, except perhaps by the most disciplined and heartless of con men. Thus when making eye contact with another, each gaze lays the other person bare. In the gaze we have the power to see each other's true intentions and desires, our deepest habits and dispositions. We can see into the very heart of our way of being in the world, even if only for a fleeting instant, even if only half consciously, and even if only partially and incompletely.

I do not think that the gaze enables the recognition of 'oneness', or a common humanity. When I look into your eyes, I see that you have your own presence, and your own identity. I recognise things about you that are similar to me and to others, but also other things that are different from me and from others. If I see a friend, or a kindred spirit, still I do not see a reflection of myself. For when I look into your eyes, I am not looking into a mirror. As Lévinas says, "the other is in no way another myself, participating with me in a common existence." (Lévinas, *Time and the Other*, pg. 75.) I think this is the point which Erich Fromm was trying to convey with his caveat that love is union "under the condition of preserving one's integrity". When meeting each other eye to eye, we engage each other in a kind of silent dialogue. That dialogue consists in the way we read each other's faces and bodies and eyes: a smile, a batting of the eyelash, a shift in the seating posture, a touch. We might be unconsciously deciding whether what we see matches with our wants and desires. But we may also be re-writing our wants and desires in response to what we see. I've a friend whose two strictest dating-rules, not to date someone without a university education and not to date someone who lives too far away, were broken immediately by the gaze of the woman he is now planning to marry.

Choice is thus still involved, and initiative preserved. But at the same time the lover who gazes on his beloved immerses himself in her presence, and loses himself in her way of being in the world.

As I gaze silently into the eyes of the red haired girl who noticed me, and as she gazes into mine, I am not yet entirely in love. But I might be *falling* there, or about to. For I am feeling a kind of magnetism in our silent dialogue. We are pulled toward each other. For the next part of the fall into love is desire. Yet it is not any kind of desire. The Spanish philosopher José Ortega Y Gasset distinguished love from ordinary desire as follows:

Desire has a passive character; when I desire something, what I actually desire is that the object come to me. Being the centre of gravity, I await things to fall down before me. Love, as we shall see, is the exact reverse of desire, for love is all activity. Instead of the object coming to me, it is I who go to the object and become part of it. In the act of love, the person goes out of himself. Love is perhaps the supreme activity which nature affords anyone for going out of himself toward something else. It does not gravitate toward me, but I toward it. (Gasset, *On Love*, pg. 10)

If I understand Gasset correctly, desire is a feeling I might have when I merely notice someone for some superficial reason. I see the attractive woman and I might briefly entertain the fantasy that she will come home with me. But I feel no gravity pulling me into her world. To fall in love, by contrast, is to feel that gravity; it is also, perhaps, to *want* to feel it. Elsewhere in his text Gasset says he prefers the idea of interest to that of desire. By this he means: when in love, we find the beloved *interesting*. I want to know more about her, I want to immerse myself in her life and her way of being in the world. Gasset also speaks of attention: "'Falling in love', initially, is no more than this: attention abnormally fastened upon another person." (*ibid*, pg. 48) Someone able to read my thoughts would see that I am thinking of fewer and fewer things besides she on whom my attention is fixed. But I, for my part, hadn't noticed that. My sense of my own presence is slowly disappearing. I haven't noticed myself noticing her: I've noticed only *her*. She is beginning to fill my world.

A special form of Revelation occurs in the loving gaze. With my gaze I reveal myself to her, but I also lay myself bare to her. The gaze is the Revelation: I look upon her as she looks upon me, and that is all I need to do to say 'I am here!' Yet this Revelation is made for not just anyone's benefit: in love I am especially interested in revealing myself to a particular person. The gaze of a lover upon his beloved is a gaze which says, 'I am here *for you*.' This form of the Revelation asserts your presence, but it also places your presence at the disposal of the beloved. It opens your being to her, it devotes your way of being in the world to her, it gives everything to her. Initiative exists here, because I make a choice to look at her or not, to let myself fall or not. But even as I possess initiative, I lose *power*. For this kind of Revelation renders you *vulnerable*. As your being is revealed *to* someone and *for* someone, so it is also exposed to manipulation, invasion, and judgment. If I invite someone into the circle of my being, I also put part of the circle of my being into her hands. I risk being changed, manipulated, exploited, rejected and humiliated, and then consigned to loneliness once more. The lover truly loves most, and best, to the extent that he makes himself open and vulnerable to his beloved. As the Sufi poet Jalaludin Rumi said, "Gamble everything for love."

Thus, to fall in love also requires courage. An element of risk is involved. Yet if she is falling in love with me too, then she presents the same Revelation of presence to me. She, too, opens herself to me with her own gaze, and makes herself vulnerable to me. And in her gaze I find a Revelation which expresses something like this: 'I see that you are here for me, that you have put yourself at my disposal. But you can trust me, for I too am here for you; I am at your disposal and I have given myself to you too.' This, I think, is the first development of a shared Revelation crafted between us: 'I am here for you, and you are here for me, and we are here for each other. And what we are, when we are together like this, is beautiful!'

Although I think this shared Revelation begins with the gaze, I also think it also requires other shared activities too. It is not enough that people look at each other: it is also necessary that they *do* things together. Thus we go on 'dates', for instance. We play games together, or make dinner together, or go to a concert together. All the while we observe each other's habits, likes and dislikes, style of communication, level of spontaneity, or tolerance for practical jokes at his expense. We talk with each other more, and no longer of polite meaningless phrases, but of our life-stories, dreams, fears, desires, ideas. We talk of the things that matter most to us. There can also be more intimate Revelations of presence in touching, kissing, and caressing each other. Should we move toward sexual intimacy, we become more vulnerable to each other still. We touch each other as closely as possible, and without the protective boundaries of skin and immune system between us. Yet if we are accepting and enjoying what we find in this dialogue, we become more trusting, more involved in each other's lives, more committed to caring for each other. The more ways that people find to reveal themselves to each other, and the more *pleasurable* those Revelations are, the deeper into love they fall.

Even so, love is fragile. At almost any time it can be interrupted. One person might unexpectedly find something undesirable about the other, which casts good qualities in a bad light. Or, one person might begin to take the other for granted, or exploit the other's kindness. Or, illusions and fantasies might arise: one person might ascribe qualities to the other which the other does not in fact possess. If this false impression should ever be dispelled, some part of the love might be dispelled with it. Love can also become enervated by too much routine. Lovers need to have regular things that they do together, or for each other, which helps establish mutual trust and reliability. But a love with no spontaneity in it quickly becomes mere 'cohabiting'. Love has to be renewed from time to time: every once in a while the lover must notice his beloved again, and fall for her again, and she with him. It is the dialogue of doing things together, formed of talking and arguing and living together, working together, touching and sexual love making, gift-giving, healing each other, and the gaze, which renews it. From this dialogue, a shared understanding and a shared *delight in each other's presence* can emerge. This delight, I think, is a Revelation; this shared delight is love.

§ 41. The Festival

Think of the songs, dances, floats, and banners, of a public parade. Think of the colours and noise of a fireworks display. These are various ways people assert their presence in public. Yet they too are configured by the peculiarities of culture, time, and place, and thus also assert a people's shared identity. The principle of the transformation of the 'I' into a 'We' is the same for two individuals as it is for neighbourhoods, communities, and whole nations.

In mediaeval Irish culture, there was a custom called 'beating the bounds'. Once a year, usually in the springtime, farm families would walk around the perimeters of their fields. One of them (usually the father) carried a firebrand, and the rest carried various noisemakers. The idea was to show themselves and their neighbours exactly where the field boundaries are, and that they need no one else's permission to move within those boundaries. It also had to do with magically warding off blights, parasites, rodents, as well as curses and evil spirits. (The participants would probably not have called it magic, but never mind that for now.) Yet I think that the tradition also asserts presence and identity too. By beating the bounds, the family shows that they are here, and that the land belongs to them, and that they belong to the land. Moreover, they show they belong to not just any land, but *this* land, which they define by the route of their walk. Finally, by Beating the Bounds people also assert their belonging to each other. In this way, the second movement of Revelation, 'This is who I am', changes into 'This is who *we are*'.

Beating the Bounds can be compared to just about any kind of public occasion where a community asserts that its people belong to a certain time and place, namely their own. It is also comparable to the occasions when people show that they belong to each other. For example, the Acadian festival of Tintamarre, (a word which means 'noise'), celebrates nothing more than the fact that the Acadian people are still alive. They are still *present* on the land that the English tried to expel them from, more than 200 years ago. During the Tintamarre parade, people dress themselves, their houses and cars in the Acadian colours (blue, white, and red, with a gold star in the blue field). They also dress in historical costumes, or any kind of crazy outfit they want. Then they make as much sound as they can, whether musical or not, with any kind of noisemaker they have: trumpets, drums, whistles, kazoos, even pots and pans. A tourism promotion pamphlet described the purpose of Tintamarre as follows: "The point is to show the world that we're still here, and we haven't gone anywhere. The point is to be heard!" In a statement like that, there's no mistaking the Revelation.

Military parades, with the colourful flags, the smart looking uniforms, and the marching bands, and so on, are one of the most visible ways that a nation asserts its presence. They also assert identity, in terms of symbolism, displayed technological power, political organization, history, social priorities, and the like. It might be an annual commemoration of the wars of the past and the soldiers who fought in them, such as a Remembrance Day parade on November 11th. It might be a display of firepower and of will, as many former communist countries used to do. Consider also a sovereignty patrol of the nation's territory. It is like a military parade, although it has different purposes: it provides a government with "total situational awareness" within its territory. The patrol might search for lost or stranded people, or it might identify and prevent criminal activity. But most of all, the patrol demonstrates to other countries that the nation is capable of moving freely in its own territory. In international law, a country that cannot do this might lose its territory to another country that can. It is thus comparable to Beating the Bounds – but with fighter jets. Sovereignty patrols of the nation's territory can thus constitute a national Revelation: it is a way for a nation to say 'We are here, and this is who we are!' Of course, the military way of saying 'We are here!' all too often takes the mode of war; fighting and destruction. The bright lights and loud sounds that assert presence and identity on a battlefield come from bombs, guns, explosions, and the engines of fighting vehicles. We've already seen the logical problem in any assertion of presence which involves killing.

But let me return to the main argument. We've seen in a previous meditation that presence reveals itself in an identifiable way. Hence why, when presence is revealed, so too is identity. Here, let it be added that this is true of communities and nations as it is for individuals. A Remembrance Day parade in Ottawa, Canada, asserts the Canadian presence, the 'We' which Canadians can say of each other. That parade offers its Revelation differently than a St. Patrick's Day parade in Galway, Ireland. And a St. Patrick's Day parade in Galway is not the same as a St. Patrick's Day parade in New York City. For any public event, there will be distinct peculiarities of cultural identity embodied in the songs, dances, instruments, colours, costumes, dramatis personae, degree of commercialism, nationalism, or religiosity. Those who participate in the 'We' expressed by these events know that they belong somewhere. The shared identity asserted by a community event tells a people that they 'have' each other, they can identify with each other, communicate and trade with each other, and trust each other. Thus they form a major part of a people's shared way of being in the world.

Let it further be added that a community, as much as an individual, is similarly bound by the requirement to assert that life is ethically desirable. This requirement, when fulfilled, is the movement which makes the Revelation complete. I think communities do this best in their regular festivals. Festivals are ways that communities *enjoy* themselves, and enjoy being who they are. Festivals celebrate the various elements of history, climate, geography, and language that bring a people together and make them who they are. Consider a gathering of modern day Druids, Wiccans, Heathens, and similar magical people. By day they hold workshops, rituals, musical concerts, artistic presentations, markets, and feasts. By night, they gather in a grove of trees, where outsiders are less likely to see them, and they build a fire. In the innermost ring around the fire, they dance. In the next ring, they play drums for the dancers. And outside that ring they talk, share food and drink, rest from dancing and drumming, meet new friends, flirt, tell dirty jokes, and laugh. There are a few rules of etiquette, such as the requirement that drummers must play the same rhythm together, and that dancers must give each other the space they need to dance safely. Dancers also move clockwise around the fire, following the sun (as seen in the northern hemisphere; they go counter-clockwise in the south). But otherwise people freely express themselves in whatever way they wish. The occasion might be an environmental transition, such as the arrival of the spring. It might be an astronomical observation, like a solstice, an equinox, or the full moon. Because the occasion is usually the observation of an organic, ecological, or astronomical event, the fire-dance celebrates embodied life, and the fact of being alive in the world, most directly and honestly.

Not only in festivals is the shared Revelation visible. It can also be seen in a society's public commons. The word 'commons' as I am using it here originates in the shared agricultural fields of mediaeval Scotland. Everyone in a certain locality was entitled to graze as many sheep and cattle on the shared lands, so long as they could house and feed those animals in their own corrals over the winter. (Thus the notion of the commons had a built-in mechanism to prevent the resource from being depleted and spoiled for everyone.) Yet the commons today can also refer to a society's organized and community-funded means of procuring certain necessities for survival and human dignity. Thus it can include public health care and public hospitals, public schools and universities, public libraries, municipal water mains and sewers, parks and gardens, democratic elections and town-hall meetings, police services, sports fields, postal services, public hiking trails in forests, building codes to prevent collapses and fires, art galleries and museums. In the services necessary for life, survival, and dignity, which a society has decided should belong to the people as a whole, administered on a not-for-profit basis and universally accessible, there you find a society's shared way of being in the world. The things included in the commons may be different from one country to the next: thus each country gives to itself a distinct identity. And this is something you can directly perceive. The siren of an ambulance, for example, is the sound of a society affirming the desirability of life by coming to the rescue of one of its members.

Yet of all these examples, I think the fire-dance is a pure-type example of every commons in the world, when it appropriately fulfills the requirement to assert the ethical desirability of life. It has all the elements of a life-affirming celebration: dancing, feasting, singing, making music and love. Something like it is what we find when, using the philosophical *epoché*, we look past the accidental particularities of any culture's holidays, to discern what remains. Then we see a whole community of people, not just a scattering of individuals, enjoying their shared life, singing and dancing around a fire. The main differences will have to do with what fire the people dance around; or to put it another way, what takes the place of the fire. Some dance for the harvest. Some dance for the end of winter and the return of spring. Some dance for the anniversary of a special event in the nation's history, such as the day the state was founded, or the day a foreign occupier was expelled. Some dance for the winning of a war; some dance for the end of the war. Some dance to celebrate the reception of a gift or a message from the gods. This is the meaning of holy days like Passover, Christmas, Easter, Yom Kippur, Buddha's Birthday, and the Night of Power. Some dance for New Year's Eve, which is really a pointless holiday since it doesn't seem to celebrate anything in particular but the day we flip over the calendar. But in terms of the Revelation it is actually rather honest. It celebrates that we are alive, that we survived another year, and that our society didn't collapse and the world didn't end. Like the fire-dance, it celebrates the continuity of life over time, and nothing else, and nothing less. But whatever else we celebrate, at the deepest root our fires also celebrate the relationships we have with each other, with the earth, with time, and with everything involved in being who we are, and being alive.

§ 42. The Artist

The discourse on Revelation could stop here, and be reasonably useful and complete. However, for other purposes, this will not be enough. To craft a way of being in the world which can transform loneliness into a source of meaning, and affirm the ethical desirability of life, we need something more. Several crucial questions remain unanswered. For instance, I have just now said that the Revelation finds its fullest expression in the ways we celebrate our relationships. Yet I also said that the values that support our relationships cannot be utilitarian in character, lest the relationship remain shallow and transient. What values remain? I also noted that the Revelation is a presence to be experienced and not a commandment to be obeyed. With that criterion in mind, what kind of an ethical understanding can there be? What kind of ethics has no rules and no laws, and yet can still tell us what to do?

I found a possible answer to each of these questions in a few unexpected places. A little while ago I was watching television highlights of great moments in the history of World Cup football. In 1995, Columbian goalkeeper Rene Higuita defended a ball heading into his net by jumping forward into a handstand, and blocking the ball with the soles of his feet. It was an amazing sight to see. And on his face afterwards was the most wonderful expression of bliss. This athlete thoroughly enjoyed the use of his body and delighted in its powers.

On another occasion, I had the opportunity to watch an elderly woodcarver making a cabinet, using only hand tools. He was patient and quiet, and went about the work slowly. He would frequently stop to just look at his work in progress, and silently think about it. Yet he had a sense of focus and total unity of purpose which was a wonder to behold. A few days later, when I saw the finished product, it seemed to me that more than just a material object was presented to me. I could 'see', so to speak, the care and the love which went into it.

Before that, I was visiting the Art Gallery of Ontario, in Toronto Canada. On display that day was a painting by Lawren Harris of an overcast sky at twilight, where each band of cloud was just slightly darker than the next one. It was a still image, made from oil-based paint on canvas, but it seemed animated: it seemed as if I could actually watch the sun set, or rise, over the land.

On one level, each of these actions was practical. A football was prevented from entering the net. A cabinet was built. A painting was sold to a patron, so that the artist could make his living. Then it was sold to a gallery, so the patron could profit on his investment. But there is more to it than that. The football goalkeeper could have just caught the ball in his hands. The carpenter could have finished his work a lot faster using machines. Lawren Harris could have painted his beaver swamp to look like a photograph, or a surveyor's map. But that is not what these people did. Another priority besides practical expediency was at work in their minds. What was it?

In the ancient Irish story of Cu Chullain's courtship of Emer, there is a list of the various skills that were taught to the apprentices at Scathach's school for heroes. Here is the list from the *Táin* itself:

So Cuchullain's training with Scathach in the craft of arms was done: what with the apple-feat – juggling nine apples with never more than one in his palm: the thunder-feat; the feats of the sword-edge and the sloped shield; the feats of the javelin and rope; the body-feat; the feat of the Cat and the heroic salmon-leap; the pole-throw and the leap over a poisoned stroke; the noble chariot-fighter's crouch; the *gae bolga*; the spurt of speed; the feat of the chariot-wheel thrown on high and the feat of the shield-rim; the breath-feat, with gold apples blown up into the air; the snapping mouth and the hero's scream; the stroke of precision; the stunning-shot and the cry-stroke; stepping on a lance in flight and straightening erect on its point; the sickle-chariot; and the trussing of a warrior on the points of spears. (Kinsella, *The Táin*, pg. 34)

This impressive list of athletic stunts which Cu Chullain and the other warrior apprentices learned from Scathach constitute technical skills for warriors. They can be compared to the outstanding acrobatics that are observed at international sporting events, and to outstanding works of art and crafts-manship as well. The Salmon Leap, and other heroic feats, were on one level practical – they got the job done – but on another level they were probably beautiful to watch. Hence, I think, why they received the theatrical names that they bear.

Similarly, in Irish custom bards and musicians were expected to have three highly specialized skills known as the Three Noble Strains: lullabies to induce sleep, laments to induce tears, and satires to induce laughter. In Irish Brehon law, the ability to perform these three types of music were expected of the *cruit*, the harper, the only entertainer in old Irish society with independent legal standing. (Kelly, *A Guide to Early Irish Law*, pg. 64) The Three Noble Strains could constitute technical skills for musicians: but they too are beautiful. We appreciate them not just because they have specific practical effects. We value them because there is something about them which gives both performer and audience a certain special kind of satisfaction. They make you feel not just that the job was done well, but that the job *had* to be done that way, could only have been done that way, that no other way of doing it would have been *right*. And we *enjoy* that feeling. Just as in the case of the football player, the carpenter, and the painter, the beauty of the action was not a matter of superfluous ornamentation. It was not 'added on' to an otherwise finished product. The beauty of the act somehow configured the action itself.

This understanding of ethics admits no rules and laws, and is not utilitarian in nature. But it is still able to tell us the difference between good and evil, and still able to suggest robust moral values to guide our lives towards excellence. Instead of defining rules and regulations, or calculating outcomes, it defines virtues, that is, comprehensive ways of being in the world which are enjoyable to practice, and delightful to see. This latter point is perhaps significant. When the beautiful and the good intersect each other, as they do in these examples, we do more than just logically infer that the person involved finds life ethically desirable. We can also directly *see* the Revelation of the goodness she finds in her way of being in the world. This proposition that life is ethically desirable is no less precise for being presented in the mode of actions, instead of in the mode of written or spoken propositions. We can do what is good or just or right *for the sake of beauty*, rather than for the sake of fulfilling duties and obligations, or pursuing calculated outcomes. We can practice certain habits and virtues because they are beautiful, rather than because they are prescribed by some authority. My working hypothesis is that when we live that way, with beauty treated as a virtue, our lives suddenly become meaningful and worthwhile.

§ 43. The Beautiful and the Good

This observation opens up new questions like, what is beauty? Why do we like beautiful things? Is there anything that ethics and ethical choices can have in common with art, and artistic choices? (So close to the end, and so many questions yet to answer!)

Already I perceive various problems. For one thing, it is not certain that all works of art have something in common with each other. It might be fairly obvious, for instance, that five hundred long-stem balloons tied up in a giant pile and dropped in the concourse of a shopping mall is not art. (I saw just such a thing as part of the 2007 *Nuit Blanche* exhibition in Toronto's Eaton Centre). Yet it may be difficult to say exactly *why* such a thing is not art. There might not be any common, uniquely definitive quality that such a thing shares with all other works of art, and only with other works of art.

We've already seen two definitions of beauty: one from the modern aesthetics of Baumgarten, and one from Plotinus and the Neoplatonic tradition. A friend of mine is an artist in Montreal, so I asked her what beauty is. She said:

"Beauty is a small meaning, fitting into a whole. An energy that radiates from within things. It requires care, awareness, attention, and consciousness. It's a quality that hits the heart. It's not rational; it's an emotional thing. And it's a physical thing: as in when we see a breath-taking landscape. It affects us in the heart." (E.R. Michaud, 2008)

What I like about my friend's account of beauty is its acknowledgement of how beauty is not just 'in the eye of the beholder'. It is also a quality of things which seems to call out to us, and which takes our breath away. Beautiful things seem to tug at our minds and feelings, and invite the senses to play upon them.

Sometimes beauty is powerful enough to compel our appreciation against our will. Many people simply cannot help themselves when they perceive a magnificently colourful sunset, a charming brook in a forest, a peaceful valley, a grand mountain. It is the same for human-made works of art, whether in galleries or on street corners or in your own home. People often find they must stop and look; they have to investigate further, draw other people's attention to it; wonder about it; and become absorbed in it. They often feel they have little choice. Whatever else beauty might be, let us at least tentatively agree that beauty is that heart-tugging, breath-taking quality.

In the last meditation I suggested that a spiritual life involves treating beauty as an ethical principle. What might that mean? If beauty can be treated as an ethical category, then can ethics be treated as an aesthetic category? If so, what might *that* mean? A relation between beauty and ethics was implied by my friend when she said that beauty requires care and attention. On the other hand, all sorts of oppression, violence, and misery could be justified if something of beauty was the intended practical result. An action which ordinary intuition would describe as shockingly violent, but which was performed with grace or flair, such as any of the Celtic warrior feats described earlier, we would have to concede might be beautiful. It's easy to imagine other examples. The grandeur and glory of Imperial Rome's architectural monuments were made possible by slave labour. The diamond importing industry continues to benefit from warfare in Africa. The textile and clothing industry still depends greatly upon the supply of cheap indentured workers in sweatshop factories in third-world countries.

A categorical contrast between ethics and aesthetics was summed up by philosopher Thomas Mann like this:

In the final analysis, there are only two basic attitudes, two points of view: the aesthetic and the moral. Socialism is a strictly moral world-view. Nietzsche, on the other hand, is the most uncompromisingly perfect aesthete in the history of thought. (Mann, *Last Essays*, pg. 172)

Thomas Mann uses the word 'socialism' here, although he is not describing a political ideology. What he has in mind is the idea that ethics is highly deontological: to him, ethics is the articulation of laws of social co-operation, founded upon reason. He refers to Friedrich Nietzsche as an uncompromisingly perfect aesthete – but he is not exactly singing Nietzsche's praise. His point is that a purely aesthetic world view has to be indifferent to the claims of morality, and that aesthetic purposes and standards are not subject to analysis in terms of good and evil. And for Mann, this is a serious problem. If morality and beauty have nothing to do with each other, it might be possible to dominate and exploit and sacrifice people for the sake of art. Insofar as the aesthetic life and the ethical life stand in contrast with each other, as Thomas Mann says they must, then the way will remain open for a Nietzschean vision where "the wretchedness of struggling men must grow still greater in order to make possible the production of a world of art for a small number of Olympian men". (*Nietzsche Werke*, pg. 261)

I think Thomas Mann's objection is rooted in a false dichotomy. There doesn't have to be a strict categorical division between the beautiful and the ethical. There are things people do which are clearly ethically desirable, and at the same time are a joy to see. Certainly, it is not just works of art which we call beautiful. We are also impressed by actions, and we are impressed by the people who perform them. Many of the most important virtues described in mythology and philosophy, such as honour, loyalty, courage, and so on, are valued not just because they produce good consequences. We also value them because we enjoy *seeing* people doing honourable, loyal, and courageous things. We feel a kind of satisfaction and delight with, for example, the sight of an underdog competitor winning a sporting competition, or a soldier on a helicopter winch cable pulling someone from a capsized boat, or a mother singing her child to sleep. We experience the same kind of aesthetic satisfaction from observing acts of compassion, or generosity, or courage, as we do observing Shakespearean dramas, or Renaissance paintings, or Romantic symphonies. Drama and literature may be particularly effective examples: we find narrative and dramatic art beautiful precisely because of the actions of the characters.

I'm not suggesting that virtue is associated with hedonism (although, as a point of historical interest, that association has often been made, especially in connection with pre-Christian Greek and Roman society). I'm suggesting, rather, that virtue is associated with *art*. In this association we may find a new way to understand Nietzsche's claim that art is "the metaphysical activity of man". A virtuous person seeks the beautiful in her way of being in the world, in much the same way that a composer seeks it in music, a writer in language, an artist of any kind in her art. For to learn a virtue is not to learn a set of rules. To learn a virtue is to learn a way of holding yourself or having yourself, and a way of presenting and revealing yourself to others. For a virtue is not a rule nor a law: it is a comprehensive way of being in the world. It involves your intelligent mind, the instincts of your belly and the feelings of your heart. It dwells in your four limbs and five senses. Once learned, it becomes part of who you are. Just as a stonemason fashions a wall, or the smith fashions a blade, or a potter fashions a jar, *so does a virtuous person fashion herself.* The same can be said of the crafting of her most important relationships. And just as an artist creates the painting, or the sonata, or the dramatic performance, for the sake of beauty, so does the virtuous person craft herself and her relationships *for the sake of beauty.*

If the four movements of the Revelation are your guides in this process, then Thomas Mann's objection should disappear. For the entire enterprise of crafting your life, your identity, and your relationships in the mode of a work of art would be guided by the principle of aesthetic life-affirmation. It would also be guided by the search for others with whom to share that affirmation. In the Revelation, the meeting place of ethics and aesthetics appears in the *desire for life* which is our most important defence against the existential loneliness of being. This is perhaps most visible in mythology: so many of the heroes express in their stories a great desire for life, *notwithstanding* that they also saw their world as such an unpredictable, precarious place, full of despair. Historian Edith Hamilton wrote that:

> The Greeks were keenly aware, terribly aware, of life's uncertainty and the imminence of death. Over and over again they emphasize the brevity and the failure of all human endeavour, the swift passing of all that is beautiful and joyful. To Pindar, even as he glorifies the victor in the games, life is 'a shadow's dream'. But never, not in their darkest moments, do they lose their taste for life. It is always a wonder and a delight, the world a place of beauty, and they themselves rejoicing to be alive in it. (Hamilton, *The Greek Way*, pg. 20)

This is a very romantic observation. Nietzsche noted it in some of his works as well. And while Hamilton thought it was distinct to the Greek world, in fact it can be found all over pre-Christian Europe, and all over the Aboriginal world too. A poetic fragment by G.K. Chesterton, in *The Ballad of the White Horse*, expresses this idea in reference to the Irish:

> For the great Gaels of Ireland
> Are the men that God made mad,
> For all their wars are merry,
> And all their songs are sad.

It would appear that Chesterton's view of the Celts was similar to Hamilton's view of the Greeks: that the Celts were a people whose talent for enjoying life could not be quelled by anything. Even the sadness of their songs is an expression of the good life: they acknowledge the total reality of life, including its miseries and losses. A culture that can turn occasions of sadness into *art* is a culture that can find the beauty of life in everything. There are enough examples of this in Celtic mythology alone that it's hard to pick which to mention here. There is Fionn MacCumhall's statement that the finest music in all the world is simply 'the music of what happens'. Another favourite of mine comes from the story of Oisin, the Irish hero brought to the Otherworld by Niamh of the Golden Hair. He returned from the Otherworld to find that in his absence Ireland had been converted to Christianity. Saint Patrick asked him what sustained his people before the Gospel teachings arrived. Oisin's answer, well known to Druids today, is "the truth that was in our hearts, and strength in our arms, and fulfillment in our tongues." (Gregory, *Gods and Fighting Men*, pg. 342.) This is not the morality of a man who humbly accepts and stoically endures whatever the world throws at him. It is the morality of a man who participates in the world, possesses and expresses himself in the world, and seeks the good in the world. It is the morality of a man who is delighted to be alive. That is the kind of morality which I think a truly spiritual person has to have.

§ 44. The Ocean

After all this work, dear friend, I'm almost ashamed to say that the centre of life created by the Revelation still does not solve the problem of loneliness. For loneliness is an existential condition of things. Thus, alas, it cannot be permanently and perfectly destroyed. It is always possible that it will find a new way to reach you. So long as things are distant from each other, they are lonely; so long as some part of that distance is inevitable, loneliness is inevitable too.

Nonetheless I have great confidence in life. Since discovering the Revelation happening all around me, I feel as if I finally live in a livable world. Almost everything around me has a presence to reveal, and a story to tell. I also perceive the ways that I participate in their stories. If more people became able to see that everything and everyone around them is openly and generously offering its presence to everything else, then people will perhaps have a means to create a better understanding of each other. If we see that each of us is also revealing ourselves to others, all the time, perhaps we will acquire greater self-understanding too. Through those two understandings, perhaps our problems and conflicts will become more manageable, less daunting, easier to solve, easier to forgive and easier to heal. We will be able to look at one another, and see what we're doing, and hear what we're saying, and know that all of us, together and apart, are just experimenting with different ways of revealing to each other the same human presence. And so we keep experimenting until we find a way that works. It's like a dance that never ends, a long, everlasting, wonderful dance, in which the music is always changing, and the steps always changing, and the rhythm is always changing, yet there is always music and always dancing going on. When we see that we are all adrift in the same ocean of loneliness, yet all the while we are showing the same message of presence to each other, then perhaps we will become closer to each other. More than that, perhaps the lives that we live, together and apart, will be more satisfying and worthwhile, for ourselves and for each other, and for all of life on Earth.

§ 45. The Turning of the Wheel

My friend and I are folding up the blanket now, and putting our shoes back on. The concert is over; it is now time to find a pub where we can share some more wine, and share the thoughts that the concert inspired.

With music, like Beethoven's arrangement of Schiller's *Ode to Joy*, or with whatever other means we may invent to exclaim the Revelation of presence, identity, and delight in being alive, we render the world into a place that could have a history, a culture, a language, a story. It becomes a place where one could *belong*. I've used two forms of art as the paradigm examples: architecture, the most earth-bound and permanent of arts, and music, the most immaterial and immediate. In the arts, the 'I am here!' is most explicit and deliberate. But as my partner and I walk the lamp-lit path from the amphitheatre to the road, from the sacred back to the mundane, it seems to me that *almost everything we do* is implicitly or explicitly done for the sake of that Revelation. Perhaps *civilisation itself* is the enterprise of asserting presence, identity, and life-affirmation on a very large scale. It too meets and attempts to push back the isolation, the solitude, the terrible consuming loneliness of being. It begins with two people meeting each other, who together push back the loneliness a little further than each partner can do on her own. The 'We' of the 'We are here' speaks of relationships, partnerships, friends, and lovers. These relationships define themselves over time, for instance by defining who is and who is not part of the relationship, and what the relationship is all about. From this process emerges a shared identity, and then, if all is going as it should, a shared delight in that identity. Once the 'We' is established, and the Revelation complete, a new solitude emerges, and a new search for others begins. The people who share this life together ask again, 'Is there anyone else out there?' With that question, we two go forth and meet other friends. We bear children and create families, and form various working associations, and build neighborhoods, villages, and towns. Soon the 'We are here' designates a community. That community, as a unit, discovers and creates ways to define itself and to affirm the desirability of life. Then it discovers a solitude of its own, and commences the search for others anew. Communities reach out to other communities and together they form cities, regions, provinces, and nations. Then nations reach out to other nations, and they create peace treaties, federal unions, strategic alliances, trade agreements, empires, and civilisations. At each stage people might compete and bludgeon each other and fight to the death on the way. But the Revelation has a way of gaining a hearing. For the need to affirm life is also an existential force in our world. Even so, it is fragile, and easily disturbed. It needs to be maintained and re-affirmed whenever it seems that loneliness, and the irrational or hurtful things we do to avoid loneliness, might overwhelm it. Moreover, as each Revelation resolves its contradictions and completes itself, it meets with a simple small question, prompted by loneliness, which restarts the process anew. The Revelation as a whole thus has the character of a circle, or a spiral. I look from the lights of the town before me to the light of the stars above me, and I know that all this has happened before, and all this will happen again.

The human race, as a whole, now occupies almost the entire land-surface of the earth. Our technology extends the reach of our powers to the moon and the other planets of our solar system. In this way our civilisation is beginning again the search for others on the next level. Even as you read this, deep space probes are leaving the orbit of our sun and venturing into interstellar space. They carry information about our presence and identity, our biology and DNA, and our place in the galaxy. Some carry recordings of our voices and our music. Astronomers have discovered more than 200 planets orbiting other stars. And we scan every arc second of the heavens with our most sophisticated instruments, in every wavelength of the electromagnetic spectrum. We do these things for various reasons, but a primary one is to answer the never-ending question, 'Is anyone else out there?'

Like the appearance of the high arctic to someone visiting for the first time, the universe as a whole is mostly *empty*. For most of its volume, there are perhaps only two or three hydrogen molecules or dust particles per cubic kilometer. And this emptiness is so deep that it cannot be measured: for the universe has no boundary, no centre, no top and no bottom, and no edge. I can't describe this without using the language of property-possession, and yet I'm trying to describe what the universe does *not* possess. I fall into contradictions of language again. Yet perhaps I cannot do otherwise, for the emptiness of the universe 'is' so giganormous we lack the words to grasp it. However much we measure the emptiness of space, there will always be more to measure. However far we may see with our telescopes, there will always be further reaches which we cannot yet see. The emptiness of the universe is an Immensity, perhaps the very greatest Immensity we know.

The Canadian inukshuk, the Irish portal dolman, and the deep-space radio dish antennae, are essential symbols of human life on earth, taken as a whole, against the backdrop of the entire universe. Like the cairn on the empty plain, human civilisation on planet Earth is a solitary sign of life in the cold and silent field of space. This is not simply a metaphor. Both cairns and civilisa-tions embody *the assertion of a living presence* against a backdrop of loneliness. The logic is exactly the same. The only relevant difference is the scale. As it is with individual cairns, so it is with friendships and loving couples, and so it is with civilisation itself. It too is a way of saying: 'We are here, and this is who we are, and what we are is beautiful! Is any—

Bibliography

Aristotle, *Nicomachean Ethics*, trans. Rackham, H. (Ware, Hertfordshire, UK: Wordsworth Editions, 1996)

Briggs, J. *Never in Anger*, (Harvard University Press, 1971)

Buber, Martin. *I and Thou*, trans. W. Kaufmann (New York: Scribner's, 1970)

Clark, K. *Civilisation: A Personal View*, (Harper & Row, 1969)

Collin, Giorgio (ed.) *Nietzsche Werke: Kritische Gestamtausgabe*, (Walter De Gruyter Inc., 1999)

Conrads, Ulrich (ed.) *Changing Ideas in Modern Architecture* (Massachusetts Institute of Technology Press, 1975)

Fromm, Erich. *The Art of Loving* (Harper Collins, 1956)

Gregory, Lady Augusta *Gods and Fighting Men*, (Gerards Cross, Buckinghamshire, UK: Colin Smythe, 1970 [first published 1904])

Gregory, Lady Augusta, (ed.) *The Kiltartan Poetry Book*, (Oxford University Press, 1971)

Hamilton, A. & Weil, A. *The Scalpel and the Soul: Encounters with Surgery, the Supernatural, and the Healing Power of Hope* (Tarcher, 2009)

Hamilton, *The Greek Way to Western Civilisation*, (New York USA: Norton & Co., 1942)

Hegel, *Phenomenology of Spirit*, trans. A.V. Miller (OUP 1997)

Ortega Y Gasset, José *On Love*, (New American Library / Meridian, 1957)

Joyce, *Ulysses*. (Everyman's Library, 1997)

Kant, Immanuel *Groundwork of the Metaphysics of Morals* trans. H. J. Paton (New York USA: Harper Torchbooks, 1964)

Kant, *Lectures on Ethics*, trans. Louis Infield (New York USA: Harper Torchbooks, 1963)

Kelly, *A Guide to Early Irish Law*, (Dublin: Institute for Advanced Studies, 1988)

Kinsella (trans.) *The Tain*, (Oxford University Press, 1970)

Lévinas, *Time and the Other: And Additional Essays* trans. R. Cohen (Pittsburgh, USA: Duquesne University Press, 1987)

Lévinas, *Totality and Infinity: An Essay on Exteriority* trans. Alphonso Lingis (Pittsburgh: Duquesne University Press, 1969)

Lewis Lockwood, *Beethoven: The Music and the Life* (New York: W.W. Norton Co., 2003)

Geoffrey of Monmouth, *History of the Kings of Britain*, trans. L. Thorp (London: Penguin)

Lucius Apuelius, *The Golden Ass*, trans. Robert Graves (London: Penguin, 1950)

Mann, Thomas. *Last Essays*, (Random House, 1958)

Nietzsche, *Beyond Good and Evil* trans. W. Kaufmann (New York: Vintage, 1989)

Nietzsche, *The Birth of Tragedy* (London: Penguin, 1993)

Otto, Rudolph. *The Idea of the Holy* Second Edition (Oxford University Press, 1958)

Panofsky, Erwin. *Meaning in the Visual Arts*, (Garden City, NY: Doubleday 1955)

Plato, *The Republic*, trans. G.M.A. Grube (Indianapolis USA: Hackett, 1992)

Plotinus, *The Enneads*, (Larson, 2004)

Schweitzer, *The Decay and Restoration of Civilization*, trans. Campion

Taylor, *The Malaise of Modernity*, (Toronto: CBC Massey Lectures / Concord, Ontario, Canada: House of Anansi Press, 1991)

Wittgenstein, Ludwig. *Tractatus Logico-Philosophicus* (Dover, 1998)

—- *The Nag Hammadi Library in English*, 3rd Revised Edition (Brill Academic Publishers, 1996)

BOOKS

O is a symbol of the world, of oneness and unity. In different cultures it also means the "eye," symbolizing knowledge and insight. We aim to publish books that are accessible, constructive and that challenge accepted opinion, both that of academia and the "moral majority."

Our books are available in all good English language bookstores worldwide. If you don't see the book on the shelves ask the bookstore to order it for you, quoting the ISBN number and title. Alternatively you can order online (all major online retail sites carry our titles) or contact the distributor in the relevant country, listed on the copyright page.

See our website **www.o-books.net** for a full list of over 500 titles, growing by 100 a year.

And tune in to myspiritradio.com for our book review radio show, hosted by June-Elleni Laine, where you can listen to the authors discussing their books.

9781846943553